GETTING READY FOR CHRISTMAS

25 MULTIPLE CHOICE BIBLE STUDIES FOR ADVENT

A BIBLE STUDY COMPANION BOOK TO:

GETTING READY FOR CHRISTMAS
WORD SEARCH PUZZLES
FOR ADVENT

GETTING READY FOR CHRISTMAS

25 MULTIPLE CHOICE BIBLE STUDIES FOR ADVENT

CELESTA LETCHWORTH

Fermata House
www.fermatahouse.com

ISBN: 978-1-947566-01-9
Library of Congress Control Number: 2018913562

Published by Fermata House: Versailles, Kentucky www.fermatahouse.com

Unless otherwise noted, Scripture quotations are taken from the Holy Bible: World English Bible. The World English Bible (WEB) is a Public Domain Modern English translation of the Holy Bible. The World English Bible is based on the American Standard Version of the Holy Bible first published in 1901, the Biblia Hebraica Stutgartensa Old Testament, and the Greek Majority Text New Testament.

Cover and chapter title fonts:
  Optimus Princeps by Manfred Klein.

Cover photo:
Victory Memorial Parkway_B&W by Mr. Moment, used under Creative Commons Attribution 2.0 Generic license / Cropped and flipped from original.

FROM THE
CHOOSE THIS DAY
MULTIPLE CHOICE BIBLE STUDY SERIES

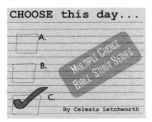

I am especially grateful for the folks that tested these Advent Bible Studies at St. James, Salem, and Marion United Methodist Churches.

ALSO AVAILABLE FROM FERMATA HOUSE BOOKS:

ℰ DEVOTIONAL BOOKS ℰ

GO AND FIND A DONKEY:
MULTIPLE CHOICE BIBLE STUDIES FOR HOLY WEEK

WAR AIN'T NO PICNIC:
30 CIVIL WAR STORIES & DEVOTIONALS

ℰ WORD SEARCH PUZZLE BOOKS ℰ

GETTING READY FOR CHRISTMAS
WORD SEARCH PUZZLES FOR ADVENT

CIVIL WAR WORD SEARCH

WORD SEARCH FOR REAL MEN
(AND WOMEN WHO ENJOY MANLY THEMED PUZZLES)

DOWNLOAD FREE SAMPLE CHAPTERS AT:

www.fermtatahouse.com

CONTENTS

INTRODUCTION

Bake cookies.
Make a list.
Shop for presents.
Hide presents.
Wrap presents.
Bake more cookies.
Address cards.
Make travel plans.
Hang wreath.
Bake more cookies.
Decorate tree.
Bake more cookies.

According to the trending magazine and online articles, this is how we get ready for Christmas. The lists have names like *Christmas Planning Tips*, *Christmas Countdown Checklist*, *Last-minute Christmas Menus*, and *15 Ways to Prepare for Christmas*. There are even summer publications advocating that August is the best time to start getting ready for Christmas.

When did Christmas become a competition, a rat race, a hectic, exhausting, stressful, busy and complicated season? According to Johnny Mathis and Andy Williams, it's supposed to be *the most wonderful time of the year.*

It's up to you and me to model an Advent posture to our children, our co-workers, and the stranger who stands behind us in the checkout lane. And it's going to take more than just saying *Merry Christmas* instead of *Happy holidays.*

All right, enough with the ranting and raving. That's not why I wrote this book.

I wrote this book to help us **get ready for Christmas** by going to the original source of the Christmas story — the Bible.

This book is designed like an Advent calendar. The daily Bible studies begin December 1 and end December 25. Each day's Scripture passages point to Christ as the reason for the season.

Use these studies personally during a coffee break or with your family in the car or at the breakfast table. They're short. They're fun. They're easy. Use them on the suggested dates, or skip around. Use your own Bible to read the Scripture passages or read them as they're printed in each chapter (from the World English Bible translation).

No need to feel intimidated if you're not familiar with some of these Scriptures — the answers to the multiple choice questions are in the back of the book. Those who have test-driven these Bible studies range from seminary graduates to those who are new to the faith.

As we **get ready for Christmas**, I pray that this book will help you focus on the Messiah, the Son of God, the Savior, the Light of the World — the ***Christ*** whose name is in the word ***Christmas***.

FAQ

How long will this study take?

Each day's Bible study should take 10-15 minutes. If you wish to spend more time each day, you could re-read the entire Scripture passage when you're finished, reflecting on your new-found understanding. If you're doing this Advent Bible Study with someone else, you could use the Meditation section as a discussion starter.

How many days will this Bible study last?

The Advent Bible Study starts December 1 and ends on December 25.

Can I do each day's study by myself, or is this just for families?

You can certainly do the Advent Bible Study by yourself. In fact, you could squeeze it in during a coffee break or at bedtime. But why not make a covenant with another person to do this study together? You could meet in person or over the phone.

Do you have any suggestions about how to use the Advent Bible Study effectively?

The directions for each day's study include — read the entire Scripture passage first. Then **re-read each section BEFORE** answering the questions. This way you will get more out of the Scripture reading. It will also improve listening skills for those around the table.

How do I know when I answer a question correctly or incorrectly?
Each question is answered in the Scripture passage immediately preceding it. Some answers paraphrase the actual Scripture, but in those cases, the correct answers are designed to be more obvious. And you can always check out the list of answers in the back of the book.

Do I _have_ to re-read the verses before answering the questions?
Yes, please. This Bible study is designed so that each day you will have read the selected Scripture passage three times — first the entire passage, then a smaller section, then re-read the smaller section to double-check your answers.

Can I use my own Bible to read each day's Scripture passages?
Sure. The verses are printed as part of each day's study, but you can read them from your own Bible instead. Just be aware that some translations use different spellings/pronunciations of people's names. For example, in Luke 1:5, John the Baptist's dad's name is _Zacharias_ in the World English Bible (WEB), and _Zechariah_ in the New Revised Standard Version (NRSV). You'll also run into minor semantics like in Luke 1:77 when the word _remission_ is used in the WEB and the NRSV uses the word _forgiveness._

I can't start on December 1. Should I wait until next year?
You can jump in anytime you want, or you can disregard the dates and use this book as 25 Bible studies. You can also skip around and not do them in chronological order — anytime there is material based on a previous day's study, you'll see that referenced.

Are there more Bible studies like this?
More studies are being developed as part of the _Choose This Day Multiple Choice Bible Study Series._ Fermata House will release the _Holy Week Multiple Choice Bible Study_ in the spring of 2019.

Your suggestions and feedback are invaluable!

Please reach out through www.fermatahouse.com.

DECEMBER 1

First read the entire passage — Luke 1:5-17.

There was in the days of Herod, the king of Judea, a certain priest named Zacharias, of the priestly division of Abijah. He had a wife of the daughters of Aaron, and her name was Elizabeth. They were both righteous before God, walking blamelessly in all the commandments and ordinances of the Lord. But they had no child, because Elizabeth was barren, and they both were well advanced in years.

Now while he executed the priest's office before God in the order of his division, according to the custom of the priest's office, his lot was to enter into the temple of the Lord and burn incense. The whole multitude of the people were praying outside at the hour of incense.

An angel of the Lord appeared to him, standing on the right side of the altar of incense. Zacharias was troubled when he saw him, and fear fell upon him. But the angel said to him, "Don't be afraid, Zacharias, because your request has been heard, and your wife, Elizabeth, will bear you a son, and you shall call his name John. You will have joy and gladness; and many will rejoice at his birth.

For he will be great in the sight of the Lord, and he will drink no wine nor strong drink. He will be filled with the Holy Spirit, even from his mother's womb. He will turn many of the children of Israel to the Lord, their God. He will go before him in the spirit and power of Elijah, 'to turn the hearts of the fathers to the children,' and the disobedient to the wisdom of the just; to prepare a people prepared for the Lord."

Now re-read verses 5-7.

> There was in the days of Herod, the king of Judea, a certain priest named Zacharias, of the priestly division of Abijah. He had a wife of the daughters of Aaron, and her name was Elizabeth. They were both righteous before God, walking blamelessly in all the commandments and ordinances of the Lord. But they had no child, because Elizabeth was barren, and they both were well advanced in years.

1. Who was king of Judea at this time?
   a) King Henry VIII
   b) King Herod
   c) King David

2. What kind of job did Zacharias have?
   a) He was a priest.
   b) He was a doctor.
   c) He was a carpenter.

3. How many children did Elizabeth and Zacharias have at this time?
   a) 0
   b) 1
   c) 5

Here's some background before you re-read verses 8-10:

In those days, one priest was chosen to enter the temple and give the offering to God while the people and the other priests waited outside and prayed. The priest was chosen by lot. Here we read that Zacharias was the chosen priest that day.

Now re-read verses 8-10.

> Now while he executed the priest's office before God in the order of his division, according to the custom of the priest's office, his lot was to enter into the temple of the Lord and burn incense. The whole multitude of the people were praying outside at the hour of incense.

1. What did Zacharias burn when he went into the temple of the Lord?
   a. toast
   b. incense
   c. trash

2. What were the people doing while they waited outside?
   a. playing soccer
   b. shouting
   c. praying

Now re-read verses 11-14.

> An angel of the Lord appeared to him, standing on the right side of the altar of incense. Zacharias was troubled when he saw him, and fear fell upon him. But the angel said to him, "Don't be afraid, Zacharias, because your request has been heard, and your wife, Elizabeth, will bear you a son, and you shall call his name John. You will have joy and gladness; and many will rejoice at his birth.

1. Who came into the temple to talk to Zacharias?
   a) Another priest
   b) An angel
   c) Elizabeth

2. Why do you think Zacharias was afraid?
   a) He heard people outside the temple screaming at him.
   b) Zacharias has always been afraid of the dark.
   c) He thought he was alone and the angel startled him.

3. What good news did the angel have?
   a) Zacharias wasn't going to have to burn incense anymore.
   b) That Zacharias' prayers were answered and he and Elizabeth were going to have a child.
   c) Zacharias was going to be promoted to High Priest.

4. What does God want Zacharias and Elizabeth to name this baby?
   a) Mary
   b) John
   c) Zacharias, Jr.

Now re-read verses 15-17.

> For he will be great in the sight of the Lord, and he will drink no wine nor strong drink. He will be filled with the Holy Spirit, even from his mother's womb. He will turn many of the children of Israel to the Lord, their God. He will go before him in the spirit and power of Elijah, 'to turn the hearts of the fathers to the children,' and the disobedient to the wisdom of the just; to prepare a people prepared for the Lord."

1. What will John be filled with, and when will this happen?
   a) He'll be filled with the Holy Spirit before he's born.
   b) He'll be filled with God's love when he's baptized.
   c) He'll be filled with popcorn when he goes to the movies.

2. What will be God's purpose for John's life?
   a) To be a shepherd.
   b) To help God's children turn back to Him.
   c) To be a priest like his father.

MEDITATION:

Zacharias and Elizabeth were deeply disappointed that they had never had children. But well after they had given up all hope, God transformed their disappointment into joy.

Think about some of the disappointments in your life that God has transformed into joy.

DECEMBER 2

REVIEW (from December 1):

1. Where did we leave Zacharias yesterday?
   a) In the temple
   b) At the movies
   c) In Bethlehem

2. What was the angel's good news?
   a) Zacharias and Elizabeth are going to have a baby.
   b) Peace on earth, good will to all people.
   c) Zacharias will never have to die.

First read the entire passage — Luke 1:18-25.

Zacharias said to the angel, "How can I be sure of this? For I am an old man, and my wife is well advanced in years." The angel answered him, "I am Gabriel, who stands in the presence of God. I was sent to speak to you, and to bring you this good news. Behold, you will be silent and not able to speak, until the day that these things will happen, because you didn't believe my words, which will be fulfilled in their proper time."

The people were waiting for Zacharias, and they marveled that he delayed in the temple. When he came out, he could not speak to them, and they perceived that he had seen a vision in the temple. He continued making signs to them, and remained mute.

When the days of his service were fulfilled, he departed to his house. After these days Elizabeth, his wife, conceived, and she hid herself five months, saying, "Thus has the Lord done to me in the days in which he looked at me, to take away my reproach among men."

Now re-read verses 18-20.

> Zacharias said to the angel, "How can I be sure of this? For I am an old man, and my wife is well advanced in years." The angel answered him, "I am Gabriel, who stands in the presence of God. I was sent to speak to you, and to bring you this good news. Behold, you will be silent and not able to speak, until the day that these things will happen, because you didn't believe my words, which will be fulfilled in their proper time."

1. What is the angel's name?
   a) Raphael
   b) Michael
   c) Gabriel

2. What was Zacharias' big mistake?
   a) He didn't believe the angel of the Lord.
   b) He forgot to burn the offering of incense.
   c) He refused to name the baby "John".

3. Why did Zacharias think he and Elizabeth could not have a baby?
   a) They were both too old.
   b) He thought they were cursed.
   c) Jewish priests can't have children.

Now re-read verses 21-22.

> The people were waiting for Zacharias, and they marveled that he delayed in the temple. When he came out, he could not speak to them, and they perceived that he had seen a vision in the temple. He continued making signs to them, and remained mute.

1. What happened to Zacharias?
   a) He can't see.
   b) He can't talk.
   c) He can't hear.

Now re-read verses 23-25.

> When the days of his service were fulfilled, he departed to his house. After these days Elizabeth, his wife, conceived, and she hid herself five months, saying, "Thus has the Lord done to me in the days in which he looked at me, to take away my reproach among men."

1. What happens to Elizabeth?
   a) She becomes pregnant.
   b) She loses her job.
   c) She moves into a new house.

MEDITATION:

At first, Zacharias doubted God's promise that he and Elizabeth would have a child. But God fulfilled that promise anyway.

Think about times in your life when you have doubted God's promises, but God has fulfilled His promises despite your doubts.

December 3

First read the entire passage — Luke 1:26-38.

Now in the sixth month, the angel Gabriel was sent from God to a city of Galilee, named Nazareth, to a virgin pledged to be married to a man whose name was Joseph, of David's house. The virgin's name was Mary.

Having come in, the angel said to her, "Rejoice, you highly favored one! The Lord is with you. Blessed are you among women!" But when she saw him, she was greatly troubled at the saying, and considered what kind of salutation this might be. The angel said to her, "Don't be afraid, Mary, for you have found favor with God. Behold, you will conceive in your womb, and give birth to a son, and will call his name 'Jesus.' He will be great, and will be called the Son of the Most High. The Lord God will give him the throne of his father, David, and he will reign over the house of Jacob forever. There will be no end to his Kingdom."

Mary said to the angel, "How can this be, seeing I am a virgin?" The angel answered her, "The Holy Spirit will come on you, and the power of the Most High will overshadow you. Therefore also the holy one who is born from you will be called the Son of God.

Behold, Elizabeth, your relative, also has conceived a son in her old age; and this is the sixth month with her who was called barren. For nothing spoken by God is impossible." Mary said, "Behold, the servant of the Lord; let it be done to me according to your word." The angel departed from her.

Now re-read verses 26-27

> Now in the sixth month, the angel Gabriel was sent from God to a city of Galilee, named Nazareth, to a virgin pledged to be married to a man whose name was Joseph, of David's house. The virgin's name was Mary.

1. Who does Gabriel visit this time?
   a) Mary
   b) Joseph
   c) David

2. Are Mary and Joseph married?
   a) Yes — for 6 months.
   b) No — only engaged.
   c) No — they haven't met yet.

3. What famous ancestor is on Joseph's family tree?
   a) King David
   b) King Herod
   c) George Washington

Now re-read verses 28-33.

> Having come in, the angel said to her, "Rejoice, you highly favored one! The Lord is with you. Blessed are you among women!" But when she saw him, she was greatly troubled at the saying, and considered what kind of salutation this might be. The angel said to her, "Don't be afraid, Mary, for you have found favor with God. Behold, you will conceive in your womb, and give birth to a son, and will call his name 'Jesus.' He will be great, and will be called the Son of the Most High. The Lord God will give him the throne of his father, David, and he will reign over the house of Jacob forever. There will be no end to his Kingdom."

1. What is Gabriel's news for Mary?
   a) She's going to have a baby.
   b) She and Joseph will never marry.
   c) Mary's mother is going to give Mary a new baby brother.

2. What does God want Mary to name the baby?
   a) Jesus
   b) Joseph
   c) John

3. What will Mary's baby be when he grows up?
   a) Doctor
   b) Soldier
   c) King

Now re-read verses 34-35.

> Mary said to the angel, "How can this be, seeing I am a virgin?"
> The angel answered her, "The Holy Spirit will come on you, and
> the power of the Most High will overshadow you. Therefore also
> the holy one who is born from you will be called the Son of God.

1. Why does Mary think she cannot have a baby?
   a) She is too old.
   b) She is still a virgin.
   c) She is too young.

2. How will Mary be able to have this baby?
   a) She will have to adopt him.
   b) Elizabeth and Zacharias will give her their baby.
   c) God will perform a miracle.

3. Whose son will Jesus be?
   a) God's son
   b) Elizabeth's son
   c) Joseph's son

Now re-read verses 36-38.

> Behold, Elizabeth, your relative, also has conceived a son in her
> old age; and this is the sixth month with her who was called barren.
> For nothing spoken by God is impossible." Mary said, "Behold, the
> servant of the Lord; let it be done to me according to your word."
> The angel departed from her.

1. Complete this sentence: "Nothing will be impossible with ___."
   a) Gabriel
   b) My own strength
   c) God

2. What is Mary's final word to Gabriel?
   a) Okay, whatever God wants — I'll do it.
   b) Okay, but first I have to talk it over with Joseph.
   c) Give me some time to think this over — I could get in big trouble, you know.

MEDITATION:

Remember today that "Nothing is impossible with God."

DECEMBER 4

First read the entire passage — Isaiah 9:6-7.

> For to us a child is born. To us a son is given; and the government will be on his shoulders. His name will be called Wonderful, Counselor, Mighty God, Everlasting Father, Prince of Peace.
>
> Of the increase of his government and of peace there shall be no end, on David's throne, and on his kingdom, to establish it, and to uphold it with justice and with righteousness from that time on, even forever. The zeal of Yahweh of Armies will perform this.

Now re-read verse 6.

> For to us a child is born. To us a son is given; and the government will be on his shoulders. His name will be called Wonderful, Counselor, Mighty God, Everlasting Father, Prince of Peace.

1. Who do you think this child is?
   a) Jesus
   b) Elvis
   c) Elizabeth

Isn't it amazing that God told Isaiah about Jesus 700 years before Jesus was born?! This is called a "PROPHECY."

A person who receives a prophecy from God is a "PROPHET." That's why we refer to Isaiah as "Isaiah the Prophet."

2. The Hebrew people thought of a name as more than just a word to call someone. They thought that a person's name described that person. In verse 6, Isaiah uses names to describe Jesus. What are they?
   a) Wonderful, Counselor, Mighty God, Everlasting Father, Prince of Peace.
   b) Wonderful, Counselor, God, Peaceful ruler.
   c) Wonderful, Terrific, Neat, Wow!

Now re-read verse 7.

> Of the increase of his government and of peace there shall be no end, on David's throne, and on his kingdom, to establish it, and to uphold it with justice and with righteousness from that time on, even forever. The zeal of Yahweh of Armies will perform this.

1. What does this verse talk about?
   a) What the world will be like when Herod is king.
   b) What the world will be like when Jesus is King.
   c) Mary and Joseph on the road to Bethlehem.

2. How will this happen?
   a) The zeal of the Lord will accomplish this.
   b) Mary will accomplish this.
   c) Zacharias' son, John, will accomplish this.

MEDITATION:

Think about your own name and what it means to you.

Then meditate on the name of JESUS and think about what that means to you.

DECEMBER 5

REVIEW

You might want to read Luke 1:35-37 and Luke1:13 to refresh your memory.

> Luke 1:35-37
> The angel answered her, "The Holy Spirit will come on you, and the power of the Most High will overshadow you. Therefore also the holy one who is born from you will be called the Son of God. Behold, Elizabeth, your relative, also has conceived a son in her old age; and this is the sixth month with her who was called barren. For nothing spoken by God is impossible."

> Luke 1:13
> But the angel said to him, "Don't be afraid, Zacharias, because your request has been heard, and your wife, Elizabeth, will bear you a son, and you shall call his name John.

1. What did the angel tell Mary?
   a) That she will be the mother of the Son of God.
   b) That she should not marry Joseph.
   c) That she won the $1,000,000.00 sweepstakes.

2. What else did the angel tell Mary?
   a) That she will have a big family.
   b) That the wise men will bring her gifts.
   c) That her relative, Elizabeth, is going to have a son.

3. Who is Elizabeth's husband?
   a) Zacharias
   b) Herod
   c) Moses

4. What will be the name of Elizabeth's son?
   a) Paul
   b) John
   c) Noah

First read the entire passage — Luke 1:39-45.

Mary arose in those days and went into the hill country with haste, into a city of Judah, and entered into the house of Zacharias and greeted Elizabeth. When Elizabeth heard Mary's greeting, the baby leaped in her womb, and Elizabeth was filled with the Holy Spirit.

She called out with a loud voice, and said, "Blessed are you among women, and blessed is the fruit of your womb! Why am I so favored, that the mother of my Lord should come to me? For behold, when the voice of your greeting came into my ears, the baby leaped in my womb for joy! Blessed is she who believed, for there will be a fulfillment of the things which have been spoken to her from the Lord!"

Now re-read verses 39-41.

Mary arose in those days and went into the hill country with haste, into a city of Judah, and entered into the house of Zacharias and greeted Elizabeth. When Elizabeth heard Mary's greeting, the baby leaped in her womb, and Elizabeth was filled with the Holy Spirit.

1. Where did Mary go?
   a) She went to see Joseph.
   b) She went to see Elizabeth.
   c) She went to see the king.

2. What happened to Elizabeth when Mary arrived?
   a) The angel visited her.
   b) She fell down.
   c) She was filled with the Holy Spirit.

Now re-read verses 42-45.

> She called out with a loud voice, and said, "Blessed are you among women, and blessed is the fruit of your womb! Why am I so favored, that the mother of my Lord should come to me? For behold, when the voice of your greeting came into my ears, the baby leaped in my womb for joy! Blessed is she who believed, for there will be a fulfillment of the things which have been spoken to her from the Lord!"

1. What does Elizabeth say about Mary?
   a) Mary is lucky to be engaged to a Godly man like Joseph.
   b) God has blessed Mary in a very special way.
   c) Mary makes the best apple pie in all of Galilee.

2. Why is Mary blessed (blessed means "happy")?
   a) She is excited about her wedding.
   b) She believed God's promise that she will be the mother of God's son.
   c) She is flattered that Elizabeth thinks she's the best cook in Galilee.

MEDITATION:

In this episode, Elizabeth is excited about the blessings that Mary has received.

The next time a friend or relative of yours receives some special blessing or good news, act like Elizabeth did and let them know you're excited for them and share in their happiness.

December 6

First read the entire passage — Luke 1:46-56.

Mary said, "My soul magnifies the Lord.

My spirit has rejoiced in God my Savior, for he has looked at the humble state of his servant. For behold, from now on, all generations will call me blessed. For he who is mighty has done great things for me. Holy is his name.

His mercy is for generations of generations on those who fear him. He has shown strength with his arm. He has scattered the proud in the imagination of their hearts. He has put down princes from their thrones. And has exalted the lowly. He has filled the hungry with good things. He has sent the rich away empty.

He has given help to Israel, his servant, that he might remember mercy, As he spoke to our fathers, to Abraham and his offspring forever." Mary stayed with her about three months, and then returned to her house.

Now re-read verse 46.

Mary said, "My soul magnifies the Lord."

1. Who is speaking here?
   a) Elizabeth
   b) Mary
   c) Joseph

2. To whom is she speaking? (You may need to re-read verses 39-45 from December 5 to refresh your memory.)
   a) Elizabeth
   b) Mary
   c) Joseph

3. How does she start her speech?
   a) She thanks Elizabeth for her kind remarks.
   b) She praises God.
   c) She cries because she does not want to be a mother.

Now re-read verses 47-49.

> My spirit has rejoiced in God my Savior, for he has looked at the humble state of his servant. For behold, from now on, all generations will call me blessed. For he who is mighty has done great things for me. Holy is his name.

1. Mary says that people from all future generations will think of her as _____ [fill in the blank].
   a) The wife of Joseph.
   b) The relative of Elizabeth.
   c) The one whom God blessed.

2. What, according to Mary, has God done?
   a) God has been terrific to her and has done wonderful things for her.
   b) God has provided fish and bread for her at every meal.
   c) God has given her a wonderful family.

3. What does Mary say God's name is? (Remember back then a person's name described that person.)
   a) Neat
   b) Powerful
   c) Holy

Now re-read verses 50-53.

> His mercy is for generations of generations on those who fear him. He has shown strength with his arm. He has scattered the proud in the imagination of their hearts. He has put down princes from their thrones. And has exalted the lowly. He has filled the hungry with good things. He has sent the rich away empty.

1. How would you summarize what Mary says here?
   a) God rewards those who think they're better than everybody.
   b) God helps the poor and humble.
   c) God helps those who help themselves.

Now re-read verses 54-56.

> He has given help to Israel, his servant, that he might remember mercy, As he spoke to our fathers, to Abraham and his offspring forever." Mary stayed with her about three months, and then returned to her house.

1. Why does Mary mention Abraham?
   a) That's what she will name her baby.
   b) Long ago, God promised Abraham that He would send help for the Israelites.
   c) Abraham Lincoln was the King of Judea at that time.

2. How long did Mary stay with Elizabeth?
   a) Until Jesus was born.
   b) She didn't stay.
   c) Three months.

MEDITATION:

Mary praises God because through her He will bless the world.

Think of some ways that God can bless others through YOU.

Now praise Him for using you in their lives.

DECEMBER 7

REVIEW

You might want to read Luke 1:5-25 and/or look at December 1 and December 2 to refresh your memory.

1. Who is Elizabeth's husband?
   a) Gabriel
   b) Zacharias
   c) King Herod

2. What happened to her husband, and why did it happen?
   a) He can't talk because he didn't believe what Gabriel told him.
   b) He can't hear because he was ashamed to sing for the people.
   c) He can't see because he forgot to burn the incense at the altar.

3. What is Elizabeth to name her son?
   a) Jesus
   b) John
   c) Gabriel

4. What will be the purpose of his life?
   a) To be a shepherd.
   b) To help God's children turn back to Him.
   c) To marry a Jewish girl and have three sons.

First read the entire passage — Luke 1:57-63.

> Now the time that Elizabeth should give birth was fulfilled, and she gave birth to a son. Her neighbors and her relatives heard that the Lord had magnified his mercy towards her, and they rejoiced with her. On the eighth day, they came to circumcise the child; and they would have called him Zacharias, after the name of the father. His mother answered, "Not so; but he will be called John."

> They said to her, "There is no one among your relatives who is called by this name." They made signs to his father, what he would have him called. He asked for a writing tablet, and wrote, "His name is John." They all marveled.

Now re-read verses 57-60.

> Now the time that Elizabeth should give birth was fulfilled, and she gave birth to a son. Her neighbors and her relatives heard that the Lord had magnified his mercy towards her, and they rejoiced with her. On the eighth day, they came to circumcise the child; and they would have called him Zacharias, after the name of the father. His mother answered, "Not so; but he will be called John."

1. What did Elizabeth's friends want to name her baby?
   a) Rebecca
   b) Herod
   c) Zacharias, Jr.

2. What did Elizabeth tell them?
   a) Okay, call him Zacharias, Jr.
   b) No, his name will be Moses.
   c) No, his name will be John.

Now re-read verses 61-63.

> They said to her, "There is no one among your relatives who is called by this name." They made signs to his father, what he would have him called. He asked for a writing tablet, and wrote, "His name is John." They all marveled.

1. Why did Elizabeth's friends object to that name?
   a) Because "John" is too common a name.
   b) Because Elizabeth and Zacharias didn't have any relatives named John.
   c) Because they like the name "Bubba" better.

2. Why did Zacharias write the name down?
   a) Because he couldn't speak.
   b) So they could see how the baby's name would be spelled.
   c) So Elizabeth wouldn't hear him.

MEDITATION:

Zacharias and Elizabeth went against the pressure of their family and friends when they named their son "John." But in so doing, they obeyed God.

Sometimes it is necessary for us to resist peer pressure in order to obey God's will.

Can you think of ways that you have resisted peer pressure in order to obey God?

DECEMBER 8

You might want to read Luke 1:59-63 and/or look at December 7 to refresh your memory.

> On the eighth day, they came to circumcise the child; and they would have called him Zacharias, after the name of the father. His mother answered, "Not so; but he will be called John." They said to her, "There is no one among your relatives who is called by this name." They made signs to his father, what he would have him called. He asked for a writing tablet, and wrote, "His name is John." They all marveled.

1. How did Zacharias let his friends know that the baby's name would be "John"?
   a. He whispered the name "John."
   b. He wrote the name "John" on a writing tablet.
   c. He spelled out "J-O-H-N" using macaroni and popsicle sticks.

First read the entire passage — Luke 1:64-75.

> His mouth was opened immediately, and his tongue freed, and he spoke, blessing God. Fear came on all who lived around them, and all these sayings were talked about throughout all the hill country of Judea. All who heard them laid them up in their heart, saying, "What then will this child be?" The hand of the Lord was with him.

> His father, Zacharias, was filled with the Holy Spirit, and prophesied, saying, "Blessed be the Lord, the God of Israel, for he has visited and redeemed his people; and has raised up a horn of salvation for us in the house of his servant David

(as he spoke by the mouth of his holy prophets who have been from of old), salvation from our enemies, and from the hand of all who hate us; to show mercy towards our fathers, to remember his holy covenant, the oath which he spoke to Abraham, our father, to grant to us that we, being delivered out of the hand of our enemies, should serve him without fear, In holiness and righteousness before him all the days of our life.

Now re-read verses 64-66.

His mouth was opened immediately, and his tongue freed, and he spoke, blessing God. Fear came on all who lived around them, and all these sayings were talked about throughout all the hill country of Judea. All who heard them laid them up in their heart, saying, "What then will this child be?" The hand of the Lord was with him.

1. What happened after Zacharias told the people what to name his baby?
   a) He danced with the baby and Elizabeth.
   b) The angel came and baptized the baby.
   c) Zacharias was able to speak again.

2. What did Zacharias do after that?
   a) He praised God.
   b) He baptized his baby.
   c) He went to the hospital to see the baby.

3. What did the people think about the baby?
   a) He's just an ordinary baby.
   b) The Lord is certainly with him.
   c) He's cute and cuddly.

Now re-read verses 67-69.

His father, Zacharias, was filled with the Holy Spirit, and prophesied, saying, "Blessed be the Lord, the God of Israel, for he has visited and redeemed his people; and has raised up a horn of salvation for us in the house of his servant David

1. Whose father is speaking here?
   a) John's
   b) Elizabeth's
   c) Mary's

2. Why is Zacharias praising God?
   a) Zacharias wanted a baby boy.
   b) God is providing the Israelites with a person who will save them and set them free.
   c) Zacharias wants to be selected to burn the incense at the altar again.

3. This deliverer will be a descendant of whom?
   a) King David, who killed Goliath.
   b) Davey Crockett, the pioneer.
   c) Amos, the prophet.

4. Who do you think this deliverer is?
   a) Adam
   b) Jesus
   c) Noah

Now re-read verses 70-75.

(as he spoke by the mouth of his holy prophets who have been from of old), salvation from our enemies, and from the hand of all who hate us; to show mercy towards our fathers, to remember his holy covenant, the oath which he spoke to Abraham, our father, to grant to us that we, being delivered out of the hand of our enemies, should serve him without fear, in holiness and righteousness before him all the days of our life.

1. Why did God promise to deliver the Israelites from their enemies?
   a) He didn't want to have to destroy the earth with another flood.
   b) He didn't like their enemies anyway.
   c) So that they would be free to serve Him without fear.

2. To whom did God make this promise?
   a) Abraham
   b) Isaac
   c) Jacob

MEDITATION:

The message of Zacharias' prophecy is that God will deliver His people from sin and oppression.

Think about the evil circumstances of our world, and remember God's promise of deliverance.

DECEMBER 9

REVIEW

You might want to read Luke 1:67-75 from December 8 to refresh your memory.

1. This first part of Zacharias' prophecy talks about:
   a) God has given up on the world.
   b) God will send us a deliverer.
   c) God made a rainbow as His promise.

First read the entire passage — Luke 1:76-80.

> And you, child, will be called a prophet of the Most High, for you will go before the face of the Lord to prepare his ways,
>
> to give knowledge of salvation to his people by the remission of their sins, because of the tender mercy of our God, whereby the dawn from on high will visit us, to shine on those who sit in darkness and the shadow of death; to guide our feet into the way of peace." The child was growing, and becoming strong in spirit, and was in the desert until the day of his public appearance to Israel.

Now re-read verse 76.

> And you, child, will be called a prophet of the Most High, for you will go before the face of the Lord to prepare his ways,

1. In this second part of Zacharias' prophecy, he talks about someone other than the Deliverer. Who is the child Zacharias is referring to now?
   a) His son, John
   b) Adam's son, Cain
   c) Boaz's son, Obed

2. What shall this child be when he grows up?
   a) A doctor
   b) A priest
   c) A prophet of the Lord

3. What will be this child's purpose in life?
   a) To prepare the way for our Lord Jesus.
   b) To heal the sick and feed the poor.
   c) To be a country western singer.

Now re-read verses 77-80.

Here's some notes to help you understand verses 77-80 better:

Remission means cancellation, or forgiveness.

(In the Lord's Prayer, we pray *forgive us our trespasses.* Some churches use the phrase, *forgive us our debts.*)

When God forgives us of our sins, our sins are cancelled out.

> to give knowledge of salvation to his people by the remission of their sins, because of the tender mercy of our God, whereby the dawn from on high will visit us, to shine on those who sit in darkness and the shadow of death; to guide our feet into the way of peace." The child was growing, and becoming strong in spirit, and was in the desert until the day of his public appearance to Israel.

1. What makes it possible for us to have our sins forgiven?
   a) We do good things for people in order to make up for our sins.
   b) God has mercy on us.
   c) It's not possible for us to ever be forgiven of our sins.

2. What else will God's mercy enable us to do?
   a) Heal the sick and feed the poor.
   b) Sing in the choir.
   c) Live in peace.

3. What happened to John when he grew up?
   a) He went to seminary to learn to be a minister.
   b) He got strong in the Spirit of the Lord.
   c) He went to medical school to learn to be a doctor.

MEDITATION:

Here's an easy way to remember the definitions of God's grace and God's mercy:

> GRACE — God gives us that which we do not deserve.
> MERCY — God does not give us that which we do deserve.

Think of one example of God's grace in your life.

Now think of one example of God's mercy in your life.

DECEMBER 10

First read the entire passage — Luke 3:1-6.

> Now in the fifteenth year of the reign of Tiberius Caesar, Pontius Pilate being governor of Judea, and Herod being tetrarch of Galilee, ... the word of God came to John, the son of Zacharias, in the wilderness.
>
> He came into all the region around the Jordan, preaching the baptism of repentance for remission of sins.
>
> As it is written in the book of the words of Isaiah the prophet, "The voice of one crying in the wilderness, 'Make ready the way of the Lord. Make his paths straight. Every valley will be filled. Every mountain and hill will be brought low. The crooked will become straight, and the rough ways smooth. All flesh will see God's salvation.'"

Now re-read verses 1-2.

> Now in the fifteenth year of the reign of Tiberius Caesar, Pontius Pilate being governor of Judea, and Herod being tetrarch of Galilee, ... the word of God came to John, the son of Zacharias, in the wilderness.

1. Who was governor of Judea at this time?
   a) Zacharias
   b) Pontius Pilate
   c) Ronald Reagan

2. Who is the main character in this Scripture passage?
   a) John the Baptist
   b) Jesus the Messiah
   c) Mary the Blessed Mother

3. Who is the main character's father?
   a) David
   b) Zacharias
   c) Isaiah

Now re-read verse 3.

Here's some notes to help you understand verse 3 better:

Repent means to do an "about face" on your sins; to turn away from your sins. It does not just mean to be sorry you sinned.

It's important to be sorry, but true repentance involves a definite action as well.

Remember in the study for December 9, we discussed what *remission* means.

> He came into all the region around the Jordan, preaching the baptism of repentance for remission of sins.

1. What purpose does John think baptism has?
   a) John baptized people who wanted to see angels.
   b) John baptized people who wanted to show that they could swim.
   c) John baptized people who wanted to show that they were repenting of their sins.

2. Why did the people want to receive the baptism of repentance from John?
   a) So their sins would be forgiven.
   b) Because everyone else was doing it.
   c) This was required by Jewish Law.

Now re-read verses 4-6.

> As it is written in the book of the words of Isaiah the prophet, "The voice of one crying in the wilderness, 'Make ready the way of the Lord. Make his paths straight. Every valley will be filled. Every mountain and hill will be brought low. The crooked will become straight, and the rough ways smooth. All flesh will see God's salvation.'"

1. From which book in the Bible are these verses quoted?
   a) Genesis
   b) Matthew
   c) Isaiah

2. Why does Luke quote these verses here?
   a) They are Luke's favorite Bible verses.
   b) John's life fulfills this prophecy.
   c) No one knows why these verses are quoted here.

3. These verses talk about John preparing a road for the arrival of our deliverer. What must he do to the rough parts of the road?
   a) He must destroy those parts of the road.
   b) He must smooth them out.
   c) Nothing — he likes bumpy roads.

4. What do you think these rough parts represent in the roads of our lives?
   a) Potholes on the Interstate highways
   b) Loneliness, guilt and lack of hope
   c) The Appalachian Mountains

5. After all this spiritual construction work is done on the highways of our lives, what will we all see?
   a) God's promise in the form of rainbow
   b) God's salvation and deliverance
   c) Christmas trees and Santa Claus

MEDITATION:

John the Baptist says that he has come to prepare the way of the Lord.

How can YOU prepare the way of our Lord in your life, your family, and your world?

December 11

First read the entire passage — Luke 3:7-17.

He said therefore to the multitudes who went out to be baptized by him, "You offspring of vipers, who warned you to flee from the wrath to come? Therefore produce fruits worthy of repentance, and don't begin to say among yourselves, 'We have Abraham for our father;' for I tell you that God is able to raise up children to Abraham from these stones!

Even now the ax also lies at the root of the trees. Every tree therefore that doesn't produce good fruit is cut down, and thrown into the fire." The multitudes asked him, "What then must we do?" He answered them, "He who has two coats, let him give to him who has none. He who has food, let him do likewise."

Tax collectors also came to be baptized, and they said to him, "Teacher, what must we do?" He said to them, "Collect no more than that which is appointed to you." Soldiers also asked him, saying, "What about us? What must we do?" He said to them, "Extort from no one by violence, neither accuse anyone wrongfully. Be content with your wages."

As the people were in expectation, and all men reasoned in their hearts concerning John, whether perhaps he was the Christ, John answered them all, "I indeed baptize you with water, but he comes who is mightier than I, the strap of whose sandals I am not worthy to loosen. He will baptize you in the Holy Spirit and fire, whose fan is in his hand, and he will thoroughly cleanse his threshing floor, and will gather the wheat into his barn; but he will burn up the chaff with unquenchable fire."

Now re-read verses 7-8.

> He said therefore to the multitudes who went out to be baptized by him, "You offspring of vipers, who warned you to flee from the wrath to come? Therefore produce fruits worthy of repentance, and don't begin to say among yourselves, 'We have Abraham for our father;' for I tell you that God is able to raise up children to Abraham from these stones!

1. What do you think John was saying when he told the people they were snakes?
    a) I wish everyone was like you!
    b) You people are no good!
    c) I'd like to take you home with me as my pets!

2. Why was John angry with the people?
    a) They continued to sin.
    b) They had a party and didn't invite him.
    c) They built a golden calf and worshipped it.

3. Why did the people think they could get away with anything?
    a) They're descendants of Abraham, whom God blessed.
    b) They're descendants of David, who killed Goliath.
    c) They thought God didn't care if they sinned or not.

Now re-read verses 9-11.

> Even now the ax also lies at the root of the trees. Every tree therefore that doesn't produce good fruit is cut down, and thrown into the fire." The multitudes asked him, "What then must we do?" He answered them, "He who has two coats, let him give to him who has none. He who has food, let him do likewise."

1. What will happen if our lives don't bear fruit? (In other words, if our actions don't show that we have a relationship with God.)
    a) We cannot be baptized.
    b) We'll have to buy our fruit at the grocery store.
    c) We'll be cut off from God.

2. What does John tell the people to do?
   a) Share what you have with those in need.
   b) Go plant some fruit trees.
   c) Go study to become priests.

Now re-read verses 12-14.

Here's some notes to help you understand verses 12-14 better:

> In those days, the people hated tax collectors because they were greedy. They collected more than the legal amount and kept the extra money for themselves.

> Tax collectors also came to be baptized, and they said to him, "Teacher, what must we do?" He said to them, "Collect no more than that which is appointed to you." Soldiers also asked him, saying, "What about us? What must we do?" He said to them, "Extort from no one by violence, neither accuse anyone wrongfully. Be content with your wages."

1. What does John say to the tax collectors?
   a) Get another type of job.
   b) Give 5% of your money to the poor.
   c) Don't charge more than the legal amount.

2. What does John say to the soldiers?
   a) Don't fight in the next war.
   b) Don't accuse someone falsely.
   c) Don't arrest any tax collectors.

Now re-read verses 15-17.

> As the people were in expectation, and all men reasoned in their hearts concerning John, whether perhaps he was the Christ, John answered them all, "I indeed baptize you with water, but he comes who is mightier than I, the strap of whose sandals I am not worthy to loosen. He will baptize you in the Holy Spirit and fire, whose fan is in his hand, and he will thoroughly cleanse his threshing floor, and will gather the wheat into his barn; but he will burn up the chaff with unquenchable fire."

1. Who did the people think John might be?
   a) The prophet (the spokesman)
   b) The Christ (the Messiah)
   c) Their new minister (the pastor)

2. John tells the people they're wrong. He says that he prepares the way for someone who is greater than he. What will this person baptize us in?
   a) Holy Spirit and fire
   b) Water
   c) Grape juice

MEDITATION:

John says that repenting from our sins is more than just being sorry — we must also change our behavior.

Think of one behavior you can change.

Now ask God to help you change it.

DECEMBER 12

First read the entire passage — I John 4:7-15.

> Beloved, let us love one another, for love is of God; and everyone who loves has been born of God, and knows God. He who doesn't love doesn't know God, for God is love.
>
> By this God's love was revealed in us, that God has sent his one and only Son into the world that we might live through him. In this is love, not that we loved God, but that he loved us, and sent his Son as the atoning sacrifice for our sins. Beloved, if God loved us in this way, we also ought to love one another.
>
> No one has seen God at any time. If we love one another, God remains in us, and his love has been perfected in us. By this we know that we remain in him and he in us, because he has given us of his Spirit.
>
> We have seen and testify that the Father has sent the Son as the Savior of the world. Whoever confesses that Jesus is the Son of God, God remains in him, and he in God.

This is from one of John's letters, not his Gospel.

The First Letter of John is followed by 2 John, 3 John, Jude and Revelation at the end of the Bible.

This is a different John than John the Baptist.

Now re-read verses 7-8.

> Beloved, let us love one another, for love is of God; and everyone who loves has been born of God, and knows God. He who doesn't love doesn't know God, for God is love.

1. What is the commandment here?
   a) Be nice to those who are nice to you.
   b) Love each other.
   c) Brush your teeth after every meal.

2. Where does love come from?
   a) God
   b) The angels
   c) Your heart

3. If you don't LOVE, then you _____
   a) don't know anything about romance.
   b) don't know the 10 Commandments.
   c) don't know God.

4. The Scripture says, "God is _____."
   a) Faith
   b) Hope
   c) Love

Now re-read verses 9-11.

> By this God's love was revealed in us, that God has sent his one and only Son into the world that we might live through him. In this is love, not that we loved God, but that he loved us, and sent his Son as the atoning sacrifice for our sins. Beloved, if God loved us in this way, we also ought to love one another.

1. What did God send us?
   a) His only son
   b) His best angels
   c) His best wishes

2. Why did God send that to us?
   a) So we can work our way to Heaven.
   b) So we might live through Him.
   c) So we can take it easy.

Now re-read verses 12-13.

> No one has seen God at any time. If we love one another, God remains in us, and his love has been perfected in us. By this we know that we remain in him and he in us, because he has given us of his Spirit.

1. What happens when we love each other?
   a) God lives in us.
   b) We get married.
   c) There won't be sin in the world anymore.

Now re-read verses 14-15.

> We have seen and testify that the Father has sent the Son as the Savior of the world. Whoever confesses that Jesus is the Son of God, God remains in him, and he in God.

1. God sent Jesus to the world to be _____.
   a) A good teacher.
   b) The one to prepare the way for the Messiah.
   c) The savior of the world.

2. What happens to you if you believe and tell others that Jesus is the Son of God?
   a) God lives in you and you live in God.
   b) God will name a star after you.
   c) An angel of the Lord will visit you.

MEDITATION:

God's greatest act of love was sending His son into our world. This Scripture says that we are to respond to this gift by loving others.

Think about some ways that your love for God can be expressed toward others.

December 13

First read the entire passage — Matthew 1:18-25.

Now the birth of Jesus Christ was like this; for after his mother, Mary, was engaged to Joseph, before they came together, she was found pregnant by the Holy Spirit. Joseph, her husband, being a righteous man, and not willing to make her a public example, intended to put her away secretly.

But when he thought about these things, behold, an angel of the Lord appeared to him in a dream, saying, "Joseph, son of David, don't be afraid to take to yourself Mary, your wife, for that which is conceived in her is of the Holy Spirit. She shall give birth to a son. You shall call his name Jesus, for it is he who shall save his people from their sins."

Now all this has happened, that it might be fulfilled which was spoken by the Lord through the prophet, saying, "Behold, the virgin shall be with child, and shall give birth to a son. They shall call his name Immanuel"; which is, being interpreted, "God with us."

Joseph arose from his sleep, and did as the angel of the Lord commanded him, and took his wife to himself; and didn't know her sexually until she had given birth to her firstborn son. He named him Jesus.

Now re-read verses 18-19.

Now the birth of Jesus Christ was like this; for after his mother, Mary, was engaged to Joseph, before they came together, she was found pregnant by the Holy Spirit. Joseph, her husband, being a righteous man, and not willing to make her a public example, intended to put her away secretly.

1. To whom was Mary engaged when she became pregnant with Jesus?
   a) Joseph
   b) Zacharias
   c) Matthew

2. What was Joseph going to do when Mary told him she's pregnant?
   a) Break the engagement and help her move out of town.
   b) Catch the next camel caravan going south.
   c) Ask her not to have the baby.

Now re-read verses 20-21.

> But when he thought about these things, behold, an angel of the Lord appeared to him in a dream, saying, "Joseph, son of David, don't be afraid to take to yourself Mary, your wife, for that which is conceived in her is of the Holy Spirit. She shall give birth to a son. You shall call his name Jesus, for it is he who shall save his people from their sins."

1. What changed Joseph's mind?
   a) He loved Mary too much.
   b) An angel talked to him in a dream.
   c) His parents made him go through with the wedding.

2. How does the angel explain Mary's pregnancy?
   a) It's a miracle performed by God.
   b) The angel has no idea.
   c) Mary's pregnancy is psychosomatic.

3. What is Joseph to name Mary's child?
   a) John
   b) Little Joe
   c) Jesus

4. What will be the purpose of Jesus' life?
   a) To build an ark and save his family from the flood.
   b) To save God's people from their sins.
   c) To run for president.

In verse 23, Matthew quotes the prophet Isaiah from the Old Testament. Read Isaiah 7:14.

> Therefore the Lord himself will give you a sign. Behold, the virgin will conceive, and bear a son, and shall call his name Immanuel.

Now re-read verses 22-23

> Now all this has happened, that it might be fulfilled which was spoken by the Lord through the prophet, saying, "Behold, the virgin shall be with child, and shall give birth to a son. They shall call his name Immanuel"; which is, being interpreted, "God with us."

1. What does Immanuel mean?
   a) Good News
   b) God with us
   c) Merry Christmas

Now re-read verses 24-25.

> Joseph arose from his sleep, and did as the angel of the Lord commanded him, and took his wife to himself; and didn't know her sexually until she had given birth to her firstborn son. He named him Jesus.

1. What did Joseph do when he woke from the dream?
   a) He did everything the angel told him to do.
   b) He asked his friends for advice.
   c) He broke the engagement and helped Mary move out of town.

MEDITATION:

Joseph thought he would be doing the right thing by breaking off his engagement with Mary. God changed Joseph's mind and showed him that Mary's unborn son was also the Son of God.

Think about times God has changed your mind.

DECEMBER 14

First read the entire passage — Jeremiah 23:5-6 (Jeremiah is in the Old Testament).

> Behold, the days come, says Yahweh, that I will raise to David a righteous Branch, and he shall reign as king and deal wisely, and shall execute justice and righteousness in the land.
>
> In his days Judah shall be saved, and Israel shall dwell safely; and this is his name by which he shall be called: Yahweh our righteousness.

Now re-read verse 5.

> Behold, the days come, says Yahweh, that I will raise to David a righteous Branch, and he shall reign as king and deal wisely, and shall execute justice and righteousness in the land.

1. God is sending the Israelites someone who will be _____.
   a) their king.
   b) their gardener.
   c) the general of their army.

2. This person will be a descendant of whom?
   a) Deborah, a past judge of Israel.
   b) King David, who killed Goliath.
   c) King Saul, the first king of Israel.

3. What kind of leader will this person be?
   a) He will be wise and fair.
   b) He will speak at least three foreign languages fluently.
   c) He will landscape the highways with beautiful wild flowers.

Now re-read verse 6.

> In his days Judah shall be saved, and Israel shall dwell safely; and this is his name by which he shall be called: Yahweh our righteousness.

1. What will happen to the Israelites when this Messiah rules as king?
   a) They will be strong and mighty.
   b) They will never have to work again.
   c) They will be safe and secure.

2. What will this person be called?
   a) The Mighty Warrior
   b) The Lord, our righteousness
   c) His Royal Highness

3. Who do you think this person is?
   a) King Herod
   b) Jesus
   c) Prince William

MEDITATION:

In this Scripture passage, God instructs His prophet, Jeremiah, to tell His people that He will send them the Messiah.

God fulfilled this promise approximately 600 years later, when He sent us Jesus Christ.

Remember that ALL God's promises will be fulfilled in the fullness of God's time.

When you get impatient, just remember — this promise was fulfilled 600 years after Jeremiah announced it. And — time belongs to God. God is never late.

DECEMBER 15

First read the entire passage — Galatians 4:4-7.

> But when the fullness of the time came, God sent out his Son, born to a woman, born under the law, that he might redeem those who were under the law, that we might receive the adoption of children.

> And because you are children, God sent out the Spirit of his Son into your hearts, crying, "Abba, Father!" So you are no longer a bondservant, but a son; and if a son, then an heir of God through Christ.

Now re-read verses 4-5.

> But when the fullness of the time came, God sent out his Son, born to a woman, born under the law, that he might redeem those who were under the law, that we might receive the adoption of children.

1. How was God's son brought into our world?
   a) He rode in on a white horse from Heaven.
   b) A woman gave birth to Him.
   c) He was born in the palace of the king.

2. When did God send us His son?
   a) When God's son asked to be sent to Earth.
   b) When God finally remembered to send Him.
   c) When God thought it was the perfect time to send Him.

3. Why was God's son born under the Jewish Law?
   a) So He could redeem those who are under the Law.
   b) Because He was allergic to ham.
   c) So He could be the general of the Israeli army.

4. Why does God's Son redeem us? ("Redeem" means to be bought at a price.)
   a) So God can adopt us as His children.
   b) So we don't have to pay bills anymore.
   c) So we can become members of a church.

Now re-read verses 6-7.

> And because you are children, God sent out the Spirit of his Son into your hearts, crying, "Abba, Father!" So you are no longer a bondservant, but a son; and if a son, then an heir of God through Christ.

1. What does God put into your heart when you become His child?
   a) The Holy Spirit
   b) The desire to become a minister
   c) A song

2. What will your heart cry out to God when you become His child?
   a) Daddy!
   b) Your Majesty!
   c) Santa!

3. The word **bondservant** means *slave*. When Jesus redeems you, you aren't a slave anymore. What are you then?
   a) A master
   b) God's child
   c) A minister of a church

MEDITATION:

Think about the difference between being someone's slave and being adopted as someone's child.

Jesus offers to purchase us from our "masters" of sin and death. This way, we can be free from this bondage and be adopted as God's children.

Think of the special relationship we can have as children of the King.

December 16

During the Advent season, we celebrate the **first** coming of the Messiah — the birth of Jesus.

We also prepare for the **second** coming of the Messiah — when Jesus will come again to establish the Kingdom of Heaven on Earth.

First read the entire passage — Matthew 25:1-13.

Here's some background before you read today's passage:

Jesus tells a parable (story) about ten young women waiting for the bridegroom to come and take them to his wedding banquet. The awaited arrival of the bridegroom represents the second coming of the Messiah.

"Then the Kingdom of Heaven will be like ten virgins, who took their lamps, and went out to meet the bridegroom. Five of them were foolish, and five were wise. Those who were foolish, when they took their lamps, took no oil with them, but the wise took oil in their vessels with their lamps.

Now while the bridegroom delayed, they all slumbered and slept. But at midnight there was a cry, 'Behold! The bridegroom is coming! Come out to meet him!' Then all those virgins arose, and trimmed their lamps.

The foolish said to the wise, 'Give us some of your oil, for our lamps are going out.' But the wise answered, saying, 'What if there isn't enough for us and you? You go rather to those who sell, and buy for yourselves.'

While they went away to buy, the bridegroom came, and those who were ready went in with him to the marriage feast, and the door was shut. Afterward the other virgins also came, saying, 'Lord, Lord, open to us.' But he answered, 'Most certainly I tell you, I don't know you.' Watch therefore, for you don't know the day nor the hour in which the Son of Man is coming.

Now re-read verses 1-4.

"Then the Kingdom of Heaven will be like ten virgins, who took their lamps, and went out to meet the bridegroom. Five of them were foolish, and five were wise. Those who were foolish, when they took their lamps, took no oil with them, but the wise took oil in their vessels with their lamps.

1. What do each of the young women carry as they go out to wait for the bridegroom?
   a) Flowers
   b) Food
   c) Lamps

2. Half of the group (five) are foolish. What do they fail to bring with them?
   a) Batteries for their lamps
   b) Oil for their lamps
   c) Matches for their lamps

3. The other half of the group are wise. What do they bring with them?
   a) A jar of oil
   b) A flashlight for backup
   c) A loaf of bread

Now re-read verses 5-7.

Now while the bridegroom delayed, they all slumbered and slept. But at midnight there was a cry, 'Behold! The bridegroom is coming! Come out to meet him!' Then all those virgins arose, and trimmed their lamps.

1. What do all ten of them do when they get tired of waiting for the bridegroom?
   a) They go back home.
   b) They fall asleep.
   c) They call him to see what's taking him so long.

2. What do all ten of them do when they hear that the bridegroom has arrived?
   a) They wake up and adjust their lamps.
   b) They run home to change into dressier clothes.
   c) They hide.

Now re-read verses 8-9.

> The foolish said to the wise, 'Give us some of your oil, for our lamps are going out.' But the wise answered, saying, 'What if there isn't enough for us and you? You go rather to those who sell, and buy for yourselves.'

1. What do the foolish girls say to the wise girls?
   a) "Give us some of your bread. We're hungry."
   b) "Give us some of your jewelry. We forgot our bracelets."
   c) "Give us some of your oil. Our lamps are going out."

2. What do the wise girls say to the foolish girls?
   a) "Okay. We'll give you some. You can pay us back later."
   b) "No. We don't have any to spare. Go buy some."
   c) "No. Our oil won't work in your lamps. You need to get newer lamps."

Now re-read verses 10-13.

> While they went away to buy, the bridegroom came, and those who were ready went in with him to the marriage feast, and the door was shut. Afterward the other virgins also came, saying, 'Lord, Lord, open to us.' But he answered, 'Most certainly I tell you, I don't know you.' Watch therefore, for you don't know the day nor the hour in which the Son of Man is coming.

1. The foolish girls leave to buy oil. What happens while they are gone?
   a) The five wise girls fall back asleep.
   b) The bridegroom arrives.
   c) It starts snowing and they can't travel back in the blizzard.

2. Where do the five wise girls (who are prepared) go?
   a) They go to the wedding banquet with the bridegroom.
   b) They go back home so they can sleep more comfortably.
   c) They go to choir practice with their Sunday School teacher.

3. What happens when the five foolish girls try to attend the wedding banquet?
   a) They get to sit at the head table.
   b) They are hired to serve food at the banquet.
   c) They aren't allowed into the banquet.

4. Jesus states the point of this parable in verse 13. What's the moral of this story?
   a) Be prepared. The Messiah could come again at any time.
   b) Always wear dressy clothes. You could be invited to a wedding reception at any time.
   c) Never trust a foolish girl with a lamp.

MEDITATION:

The Advent season is a time of preparation for the second coming of the Messiah. During this season, we remember that we must always keep watch and be ready for our Lord.

Some of the ways we prepare ourselves for the Messiah are: reading the Bible; worshipping God; helping people; telling people about God; talking to God.

Can you think of other ways we can prepare?

What can you do to be better prepared?

December 17

First read the entire passage — Matthew 1:1-17.

Don't worry about pronouncing the names correctly. People mispronounce my name all the time, and it doesn't change who I am.

The book of the genealogy of Jesus Christ, the son of David, the son of Abraham.

Abraham became the father of Isaac. Isaac became the father of Jacob. Jacob became the father of Judah and his brothers. Judah became the father of Perez and Zerah by Tamar. Perez became the father of Hezron. Hezron became the father of Ram. Ram became the father of Amminadab. Amminadab became the father of Nahshon. Nahshon became the father of Salmon. Salmon became the father of Boaz by Rahab. Boaz became the father of Obed by Ruth. Obed became the father of Jesse. Jesse became the father of King David. David became the father of Solomon by her who had been Uriah's wife. Solomon became the father of Rehoboam. Rehoboam became the father of Abijah. Abijah became the father of Asa. Asa became the father of Jehoshaphat. Jehoshaphat became the father of Joram. Joram became the father of Uzziah. Uzziah became the father of Jotham. Jotham became the father of Ahaz. Ahaz became the father of Hezekiah. Hezekiah became the father of Manasseh. Manasseh became the father of Amon. Amon became the father of Josiah. Josiah became the father of Jechoniah and his brothers, at the time of the exile to Babylon. After the exile to Babylon, Jechoniah became the father of Shealtiel. Shealtiel became the father of Zerubbabel. Zerubbabel became the father of Abiud. Abiud became the father of Eliakim. Eliakim became the father of Azor. Azor became the father of Zadok. Zadok became the father of Achim. Achim became the father of Eliud. Eliud became the father of Eleazar. Eleazar became the father of

Matthan. Matthan became the father of Jacob. Jacob became the father of Joseph, the husband of Mary, from whom was born Jesus, who is called Christ.

So all the generations from Abraham to David are fourteen generations; from David to the exile to Babylon fourteen generations; and from the carrying away to Babylon to the Christ, fourteen generations.

Now re-read verse 1.

The book of the genealogy of Jesus Christ, the son of David, the son of Abraham.

1. This is a record of the genealogy of Jesus, listing his ancestors in verses 2-16. Which two of his ancestors are also mentioned in verse 1?
   a) Joseph and Mary
   b) David and Abraham
   c) Adam and Eve

Now re-read verses 2-16. As you re-read verses 2-16:

1. See how many names you recognize.

2. Count how many women are mentioned. (Names that follow the word, "by" are mothers. For example: *Boaz became the father of Obed **by Ruth**.*)

Abraham became the father of Isaac. Isaac became the father of Jacob. Jacob became the father of Judah and his brothers. Judah became the father of Perez and Zerah by Tamar. Perez became the father of Hezron. Hezron became the father of Ram. Ram became the father of Amminadab. Amminadab became the father of Nahshon. Nahshon became the father of Salmon. Salmon became the father of Boaz by Rahab. Boaz became the father of Obed by Ruth. Obed became the father of Jesse. Jesse became the father of King David. David became the father of Solomon by her who had been Uriah's wife. Solomon became the father of Rehoboam. Rehoboam became the father of Abijah. Abijah became the father of Asa. Asa became the father of Jehoshaphat. Jehoshaphat became the father of Joram. Joram became the father of Uzziah. Uzziah became the father of Jotham. Jotham became the father of Ahaz.

Ahaz became the father of Hezekiah. Hezekiah became the father of Manasseh. Manasseh became the father of Amon. Amon became the father of Josiah. Josiah became the father of Jechoniah and his brothers, at the time of the exile to Babylon. After the exile to Babylon, Jechoniah became the father of Shealtiel. Shealtiel became the father of Zerubbabel. Zerubbabel became the father of Abiud. Abiud became the father of Eliakim. Eliakim became the father of Azor. Azor became the father of Zadok. Zadok became the father of Achim. Achim became the father of Eliud. Eliud became the father of Eleazar. Eleazar became the father of Matthan. Matthan became the father of Jacob. Jacob became the father of Joseph, the husband of Mary, from whom was born Jesus, who is called Christ.

Now re-read verse 6.

Jesse became the father of King David. David became the father of Solomon by her who had been Uriah's wife.

1. What is King David's father's name?
   a) Jesse
   b) George
   c) Jacob

Now read Isaiah 11:1-2 (Isaiah is in the Old Testament, a couple of books past Psalms.)

A shoot will come out of the stock of Jesse, and a branch out of his roots will bear fruit. Yahweh's Spirit will rest on him: the spirit of wisdom and understanding, the spirit of counsel and might, the spirit of knowledge and of the fear of Yahweh.

1. In this prophecy, Isaiah says that the Messiah will be a descendant of Jesse. How does Isaiah describe this family relationship?
   a) As a baby delivered by the stork of Jesse.
   b) As a flower from the cabbage patch of Jesse.
   c) As a branch from the family tree of Jesse.

Now re-read verse 16 from Matthew 1.

> Jacob became the father of Joseph, the husband of Mary, from whom was born Jesus, who is called Christ.

1. Who is the last man (besides Jesus) mentioned?
   a) John
   b) Joseph
   c) Jerry

2. Is the mother of Jesus mentioned?
   a) Yes. Her name is Mary.
   b) Yes. Her name is Martha.
   c) No. The mother of Jesus is not mentioned.

MEDITATION:

The list of Jesus' ancestors includes saintly people as well as those whose sins have been well documented in the Old Testament. The list also includes Gentiles (people who are not Jewish), "for there is no partiality with God." [Romans 2:11]

This inclusive list illustrates that God can restore sinners and make them part of the Divine Plan.

Think of someone you know who is an outcast. Pray for that person, asking God to help you see that person's worth through God's eyes.

DECEMBER 18

First read the entire passage — Isaiah 11:1-10.

A shoot will come out of the stock of Jesse, and a branch out of his roots will bear fruit.

Yahweh's Spirit will rest on him: the spirit of wisdom and understanding, the spirit of counsel and might, the spirit of knowledge and of the fear of Yahweh. His delight will be in the fear of Yahweh. He will not judge by the sight of his eyes, neither decide by the hearing of his ears; but with righteousness he will judge the poor, and decide with equity for the humble of the earth. He will strike the earth with the rod of his mouth; and with the breath of his lips he will kill the wicked. Righteousness will be the belt of his waist, and faithfulness the belt of his waist.

The wolf will live with the lamb, and the leopard will lie down with the young goat; the calf, the young lion, and the fattened calf together; and a little child will lead them. The cow and the bear will graze. Their young ones will lie down together. The lion will eat straw like the ox. The nursing child will play near a cobra's hole, and the weaned child will put his hand on the viper's den. They will not hurt nor destroy in all my holy mountain; for the earth will be full of the knowledge of Yahweh, as the waters cover the sea.

It will happen in that day that the nations will seek the root of Jesse, who stands as a banner of the peoples; and his resting place will be glorious.

Now re-read verse 1

A shoot will come out of the stock of Jesse, and a branch out of his roots will bear fruit.

1. Remember yesterday we read this verse that describes the Messiah as being a descendant of Jesse. Do you remember who Jesse's son is? (You may need to look back at the genealogy of Jesus in Matthew 1:1-17 from December 17.)
   a) President Lincoln
   b) Prince Charles
   c) King David

Now read Jeremiah 33:15 (Jeremiah is the book immediately following Isaiah).

> In those days, and at that time, will I cause a Branch of righteousness to grow up to David; and he shall execute justice and righteousness in the land.

1. Jesus has many nicknames, including The Good Shepherd, The Bread of Life, The Door. What is the Messiah called in this verse <u>and</u> back in Isaiah 11:1?
   a) Branch
   b) Fire
   c) Water

Now re-read verses Isaiah 11:2-5.

> Yahweh's Spirit will rest on him: the spirit of wisdom and understanding, the spirit of counsel and might, the spirit of knowledge and of the fear of Yahweh. His delight will be in the fear of Yahweh. He will not judge by the sight of his eyes, neither decide by the hearing of his ears; but with righteousness he will judge the poor, and decide with equity for the humble of the earth. He will strike the earth with the rod of his mouth; and with the breath of his lips he will kill the wicked. Righteousness will be the belt of his waist, and faithfulness the belt of his waist.

1. The seven-fold spirit rests upon the Messiah. What are the seven parts?
   a) The Spirit of the Lord, wisdom, understanding, counsel, power, knowledge, and fear of the Lord.
   b) The Spirit of Trustworthiness, loyal, helpful, friendly, courteous, kind, and reverent of the Lord.
   c) The Spirit of Cleanliness, obedient, cheerful, thrifty, brave, worship, and joy of the Lord.

2. Two qualities are so important when describing the Messiah that Isaiah says the Messiah will be wearing them as a belt and sash around his waist. What are they?
   a) Worship and praise
   b) Love and peace
   c) Righteousness and faithfulness

Now re-read verses 6-9.

> The wolf will live with the lamb, and the leopard will lie down with the young goat; the calf, the young lion, and the fattened calf together; and a little child will lead them. The cow and the bear will graze. Their young ones will lie down together. The lion will eat straw like the ox. The nursing child will play near a cobra's hole, and the weaned child will put his hand on the viper's den. They will not hurt nor destroy in all my holy mountain; for the earth will be full of the knowledge of Yahweh, as the waters cover the sea.

1. Isaiah describes Earth when it is full of the knowledge of the Lord. What will it be like?
   a) Funny
   b) Peaceful
   c) Scary

Now re-read verse 10.

> It will happen in that day that the nations will seek the root of Jesse, who stands as a banner of the peoples; and his resting place will be glorious.

1. Another nickname! What does Isaiah call the Messiah this time?
   a) Son of David
   b) Root of Jesse
   c) Bright morning star

2. Who is Jesse? (You may need to refer back to the genealogy of Jesus in Matthew 1:1-17 from December 17.)
   a) The father of David
   b) The brother of Jesus
   c) The cousin of Isaiah

3. What is the relationship between Jesse and Jesus? (You may need to refer back to the genealogy of Jesus in Matthew 1:1-17 from December 17.)
   a) Jesus is a descendant of Jesse.
   b) Jesus is a neighbor of Jesse.
   c) Jesus is an employee of Jesse.

MEDITATION:

In chapter 11, Isaiah's prophecy of the Messiah calls him a Branch and Jeremiah 33 calls him a Branch of righteousness.

Other people in the Bible have nicknames:

- They called James and John *Boanerges*, which means Sons of Thunder. [Mark 3:17]

- They called Joseph of Cyprus *Barnabus*, which means Son of Encouragement. [Acts 4:36]

What nickname would you like people to call you that describes who you are as a child of God?

Here are some ideas of Godly nicknames you might like:

- Kind Helper
- Brother of Compassion
- Sister of Patience
- Peacemaker

DECEMBER 19

First read the entire passage — John 3:16-21.

> For God so loved the world, that he gave his one and only Son, that whoever believes in him should not perish, but have eternal life.
>
> For God didn't send his Son into the world to judge the world, but that the world should be saved through him. He who believes in him is not judged. He who doesn't believe has been judged already, because he has not believed in the name of the one and only Son of God.
>
> This is the judgment, that the light has come into the world, and men loved the darkness rather than the light; for their works were evil. For everyone who does evil hates the light, and doesn't come to the light, lest his works would be exposed. But he who does the truth comes to the light, that his works may be revealed, that they have been done in God."

Now re-read verse 16.

> For God so loved the world, that he gave his one and only Son, that whoever believes in him should not perish, but have eternal life.

The Greek word for **to believe** actually means "to trust in, to adhere to, to rely on."

So — believing in Jesus is much more than accepting the fact that He exists.

Believing in Jesus means that you will allow Him to be the manager of your life.

1. Why did God give us His son?
    a) Because that was what God promised to give us if we were good.
    b) Because God loves us.
    c) Because it was Christmas and God had to give us something that we didn't already have.

2. What will happen to you if you believe in Jesus?
    a) You will live eternally with God.
    b) You will always succeed in school and in your job.
    c) Nothing special.

Now re-read verses 17-18.

> For God didn't send his Son into the world to judge the world, but that the world should be saved through him. He who believes in him is not judged. He who doesn't believe has been judged already, because he has not believed in the name of the one and only Son of God.

1. Did God send Jesus to judge us?
    a) Yes, and the guilty ones will never be allowed to attend church services.
    b) No, God sent Jesus to prepare the way for the Messiah.
    c) No, God sent Jesus to save us.

2. Who are the ones who are NOT judged?
    a) The ones who have let Jesus be the manager of their lives.
    b) The ones who go to church EVERY Sunday.
    c) The ones who have three or less speeding tickets.

3. Who judges the other ones?
    a) They judge themselves by not trusting in Jesus.
    b) The ministers and priests.
    c) Judge Judy.

Now re-read verses 19-21.

> This is the judgment, that the light has come into the world, and men loved the darkness rather than the light; for their works were evil. For everyone who does evil hates the light, and doesn't come to the light, lest his works would be exposed. But he who does the

truth comes to the light, that his works may be revealed, that they have been done in God."

1. Why do some people avoid Jesus (the Light of the world)?
   a) Because not everyone needs Jesus.
   b) Because they are the ones who will not be judged.
   c) Because the things they're doing are evil.

2. Those who do good and love Truth are not afraid of Jesus' light. Why not?
   a) Because they're members of a church, so they can do whatever they want to do.
   b) Because they try to obey God in all their actions, so they have nothing to hide.
   c) Because they have special spiritual sunglasses, so His light won't hurt their eyes.

MEDITATION:

When we think of Christmas, we usually think of gifts. But the central gift of Christmas is God's gift to us.

Read John 3:16 again.

Now think about God's gift of Jesus Christ.

Have you accepted this gift?

Have you unwrapped it? Is this gift (Jesus) a part of your life?

Martin Luther called John 3:16 the "Gospel in Miniature" because it sums up the whole Christian message.

MARTIN LUTHER
1483-1546

December 20

The Advent season is one of preparation and of waiting. The Holy Spirit revealed to Simeon that he would not die until he had seen the Messiah. In Luke 2:25-35 we read the account of the end of Simeon's waiting.

First read the entire passage — Luke 2:25-35.

Behold, there was a man in Jerusalem whose name was Simeon. This man was righteous and devout, looking for the consolation of Israel, and the Holy Spirit was on him. It had been revealed to him by the Holy Spirit that he should not see death before he had seen the Lord's Christ.

He came in the Spirit into the temple. When the parents brought in the child, Jesus, that they might do concerning him according to the custom of the law, then he received him into his arms, and blessed God, and said, "Now you are releasing your servant, Master, according to your word, in peace; for my eyes have seen your salvation, which you have prepared before the face of all peoples; a light for revelation to the nations, and the glory of your people Israel."

Joseph and his mother were marveling at the things which were spoken concerning him, and Simeon blessed them, and said to Mary, his mother, "Behold, this child is set for the falling and the rising of many in Israel, and for a sign which is spoken against. Yes, a sword will pierce through your own soul, that the thoughts of many hearts may be revealed."

Now re-read verses 25-26.

> Behold, there was a man in Jerusalem whose name was Simeon. This man was righteous and devout, looking for the consolation of Israel, and the Holy Spirit was on him. It had been revealed to him by the Holy Spirit that he should not see death before he had seen the Lord's Christ.

1. Who is Simeon?
   a) One of the three wise men.
   b) A very Godly man.
   c) The innkeeper.

2. What has the Holy Spirit promised Simeon?
   a) That he will be healed.
   b) That he will go to the promised land.
   c) That he will not die until he sees the one God has sent to save us.

Now re-read verses 27-32.

> He came in the Spirit into the temple. When the parents brought in the child, Jesus, that they might do concerning him according to the custom of the law, then he received him into his arms, and blessed God, and said, "Now you are releasing your servant, Master, according to your word, in peace; for my eyes have seen your salvation, which you have prepared before the face of all peoples; a light for revelation to the nations, and the glory of your people Israel."

The phrase *to the nations* refers to the non-Jewish nations. Many translations of the Bible use the word *Gentiles*.

When Simeon describes Jesus as *a light for revelation to the nations, and the glory of your people Israel*, he includes the Jews (*your people Israel*) and the non-Jews (*the nations*). In other words – EVERYONE.

1. Why did Simeon go in the temple?
   a) He was selected to burn incense at the altar.
   b) He felt the Holy Spirit urging him to go there.
   c) He was a member of a handbell choir that was performing there.

2. Why were Mary and Joseph and Jesus in the temple?
   a) All Jews had to take their newborn babies to the temple for a special service.
   b) It was cold, and they needed shelter.
   c) They were to meet Adam and Eve there.

3. Simeon looks at Jesus and says his eyes see _____.
   a) A little baby boy.
   b) God's salvation.
   c) The one who will build the ark.

4. What else does Simeon call Jesus?
   a) God's light for the Gentiles and the Jews.
   b) An angel of God.
   c) Baby of the Year.

Now re-read verses 33-35.

> Joseph and his mother were marveling at the things which were spoken concerning him, and Simeon blessed them, and said to Mary, his mother, "Behold, this child is set for the falling and the rising of many in Israel, and for a sign which is spoken against. Yes, a sword will pierce through your own soul, that the thoughts of many hearts may be revealed."

1. What do Mary and Joseph think of Simeon?
   a) They think he's an old, senile man.
   b) They are amazed at what he said.
   c) They are afraid of Simeon.

2. What does Simeon predict for Mary's future?
   a) She will put the baby up for adoption and she will be relieved.
   b) Things will not be easy for her and she will be sad.
   c) She will pick the right curtain on "Let's Make a Deal" and she will be thrilled.

MEDITATION:

Simeon recognized the Messiah, even though Jesus was nothing more than a helpless, little baby.

Sometimes we must look for Jesus in the most unlikely places and unlikely times of our lives.

Between now and Christmas day — see if you can recognize the Messiah working in and touching the lives of those around you.

DECEMBER 21

First read the entire passage — Micah 5:2-4

Micah is a small book of only seven chapters near the end of the Old Testament, immediately following the book of Jonah.

> But you, Bethlehem Ephrathah, being small among the clans of Judah, out of you one will come out to me that is to be ruler in Israel; whose goings out are from of old, from ancient times.

> Therefore he will abandon them until the time that she who is in labor gives birth. Then the rest of his brothers will return to the children of Israel. He shall stand, and shall shepherd in the strength of Yahweh, in the majesty of the name of Yahweh his God: and they will live, for then he will be great to the ends of the earth.

Now re-read verse 2.

Here's some notes to help you understand verse 2 better:

There were two cities in Israel named Bethlehem.

One Bethlehem was in the north, near Nazareth, in the territory of Zebulun.

The Bethlehem Micah refers to as Bethlehem Ephrathah was in the south, near Jerusalem, in the territory of Judah.

It is also called *Bethlehem in Judea* and *The City of David*.

> But you, Bethlehem Ephrathah, being small among the clans of Judah, out of you one will come out to me that is to be ruler in Israel; whose goings out are from of old, from ancient times.

1. Micah's prophesy includes the birthplace of the Messiah. Where will the Messiah be born?
   a) In Nazareth Galilee
   b) In Bethlehem Ephrathah
   c) In Dallas Texas

Now read about the quest of the wise men to find the Messiah (Matthew 2:1-6).

Listen for something familiar at the end (when the wise men answer King Herod).

> Now when Jesus was born in Bethlehem of Judea in the days of King Herod, behold, wise men from the east came to Jerusalem, saying, "Where is he who is born King of the Jews? For we saw his star in the east, and have come to worship him." When King Herod heard it, he was troubled, and all Jerusalem with him. Gathering together all the chief priests and scribes of the people, he asked them where the Christ would be born. They said to him, "In Bethlehem of Judea, for this is written through the prophet, 'You Bethlehem, land of Judah, are in no way least among the princes of Judah for out of you shall come a governor, who shall shepherd my people, Israel.'"

1. What do the Wise Men quote?
   a) Francis Scott Key's song concerning the star-spangled United States flag.
   b) Abraham Lincoln's address concerning the Battle of Gettysburg.
   c) Micah's prophesy concerning the birthplace of the Messiah.

Now re-read verses Micah 5:3-4.

> Therefore he will abandon them until the time that she who is in labor gives birth. Then the rest of his brothers will return to the children of Israel. He shall stand, and shall shepherd in the strength of Yahweh, in the majesty of the name of Yahweh his God: and they will live, for then he will be great to the ends of the earth.

1. How is the Messiah described?
   a) As a shepherd.
   b) As a race car driver.
   c) As a teacher.

Now read John 10:11.

I am the good shepherd. The good shepherd lays down his life for the sheep.

1. How does Jesus describe Himself?
   a) As The Kind Neighbor.
   b) As The Smart Teacher.
   c) As The Good Shepherd.

MEDITATION:

Micah lived in the days of Isaiah. Both prophets gave prophesies concerning the Messiah. Jesus wasn't born until about 700 years after their prophesies. Can you imagine waiting that long for a prophesy to be fulfilled?

Yesterday we read that Simeon waited a long time after the Holy Spirit promised him he would not die before he met the Messiah.

Take time now to pray for peace on earth with the confidence that your prayer will be answered sometime in the near or far future.

DECEMBER 22

First read the entire passage — John 1:19-28.

> This is John's testimony, when the Jews sent priests and Levites from Jerusalem to ask him, "Who are you?" He declared, and didn't deny, but he declared, "I am not the Christ."
>
> They asked him, "What then? Are you Elijah?" He said, "I am not." "Are you the prophet?" He answered, "No." They said therefore to him, "Who are you? Give us an answer to take back to those who sent us. What do you say about yourself?"
>
> He said, "I am the voice of one crying in the wilderness, 'Make straight the way of the Lord,' as Isaiah the prophet said."
>
> The ones who had been sent were from the Pharisees. They asked him, "Why then do you baptize, if you are not the Christ, nor Elijah, nor the prophet?" John answered them, "I baptize in water, but among you stands one whom you don't know. He is the one who comes after me, who is preferred before me, whose sandal strap I'm not worthy to loosen." These things were done in Bethany beyond the Jordan, where John was baptizing.

Now re-read verses 19-20.

The Greek word **Christ** and the Hebrew word **Messiah** both mean *The Anointed One*.

> This is John's testimony, when the Jews sent priests and Levites from Jerusalem to ask him, "Who are you?" He declared, and didn't deny, but he declared, "I am not the Christ."

1. Who do the religious leaders approach, hoping that he is the Messiah (the Christ)?
   a) Jesus the Savior
   b) David the King
   c) John the Baptist

2. What do they ask him?
   a) What are you doing?
   b) Who are you?
   c) Do you know who we are?

3. How does he answer them?
   a) No, I am not the Messiah.
   b) Yes, I am the Messiah.
   c) Maybe I am, maybe I'm not. Who wants to know?

Now re-read verses 21-22.

> They asked him, "What then? Are you Elijah?" He said, "I am not."
> "Are you the prophet?" He answered, "No." They said therefore to him, "Who are you? Give us an answer to take back to those who sent us. What do you say about yourself?"

1. These religious leaders are hoping John is someone important. Who do they think he might be?
   a) Noah
   b) Adam
   c) Elijah

2. How does John answer them?
   a) No, I am not.
   b) Oh yeah, sorry I forgot.
   c) I don't understand the question.

Now re-read verse 23.

> He said, "I am the voice of one crying in the wilderness, 'Make straight the way of the Lord,' as Isaiah the prophet said."

1. From which book in the Old Testament does John quote for his final
   answer?
   a) The Book of Jeremiah
   b) The Book of Micah
   c) The Book of Isaiah

Now read Isaiah 40:3 (Isaiah is in the Old Testament, a couple of books past Psalms.)

> The voice of one who calls out, "Prepare the way of Yahweh in the wilderness! Make a level highway in the desert for our God."

All four Gospels quote this Scripture when they describe John the Baptist. That's 4 out of 4! (Matthew 3:1-3; Mark 1:2-4; Luke 3:2-6; John 1:23)

1. How does John refer to himself when he quotes the prophecy?
   a) I am the Voice.
   b) I am the Messiah.
   c) I am the Baptizer.

Now re-read John 1:24-28.

> The ones who had been sent were from the Pharisees. They asked him, "Why then do you baptize, if you are not the Christ, nor Elijah, nor the prophet?" John answered them, "I baptize in water, but among you stands one whom you don't know. He is the one who comes after me, who is preferred before me, whose sandal strap I'm not worthy to loosen." These things were done in Bethany beyond the Jordan, where John was baptizing.

1. What does John use when he baptizes people?
   a) Olive oil
   b) Water
   c) Snow flakes

2. Where is John when the religious leaders confront him?
   a) Near the Jordan river where John is baptizing.
   b) Near the synagogue where John is preaching.
   c) Near Jerusalem University where John is teaching.

MEDITATION:

When John quotes Isaiah 40:3 he says, *Make straight the way of the Lord.*

In the highways of the journeys of our lives, we must straighten out the crooked paths of our wrong doings.

Think of a crooked path in your life that needs to be straightened.

Thank God for sending Jesus to save us from our sins and help us straighten out our crooked ways!

December 23

First read the entire passage — Luke 2:1-6.

Here's some notes to help you understand verses 1-6 better:

Enrollment refers to taking a census of the population. Each person had to register in the city where their lineage was registered. Since Joseph was of the house of David, he had to register (enroll) in Bethlehem.

> Now in those days, a decree went out from Caesar Augustus that all the world should be enrolled. This was the first enrollment made when Quirinius was governor of Syria. All went to enroll themselves, everyone to his own city.
>
> Joseph also went up from Galilee, out of the city of Nazareth, into Judea, to David's city, which is called Bethlehem, because he was of the house and family of David;
>
> to enroll himself with Mary, who was pledged to be married to him as wife, being pregnant. While they were there, the day had come for her to give birth.

Now re-read verses 1-3.

> Now in those days, a decree went out from Caesar Augustus that all the world should be enrolled. This was the first enrollment made when Quirinius was governor of Syria. All went to enroll themselves, everyone to his own city.

1. Who issued the order for a census to be taken?
    a) Augustus
    b) Herod
    c) David

2. Who was the governor of Syria at this time?
    a) Herod
    b) Quirinius
    c) Solomon

3. Where did the people have to register for the census?
    a) Each person went to his ancestor's town to register.
    b) A census-taker went door-to-door and registered each person.
    c) Each person went to the synagogue to register.

Now re-read verse 4.

> Joseph also went up from Galilee, out of the city of Nazareth, into Judea, to David's city, which is called Bethlehem, because he was of the house and family of David;

1. Where was Joseph when he heard the news about the census?
    a) In the town of Philadelphia in Pennsylvania.
    b) In the town of Nazareth in Galilee.
    c) In the town of Jerusalem in Judea.

2. Where does Joseph have to go for the census?
    a) To the town of Bethlehem in Judea.
    b) To the town of Jericho in Judea.
    c) To the town of Bethlehem in Pennsylvania.

3. Why does Joseph have to go there to register?
    a) Because there was no room at the inn.
    b) Because someone misfiled his information in Nazareth.
    c) Because he's a descendant of David.

Now re-read verses 5-6.

> to enroll himself with Mary, who was pledged to be married to him as wife, being pregnant. While they were there, the day had come for her to give birth.

1. What did Mary do during the census?
   a) She stayed in Nazareth and registered there.
   b) She went with Joseph to register in Bethlehem.
   c) She went to stay with Elizabeth again.

2. What medical condition does Mary have during their journey?
   a) She pulled a hamstring because she forgot to stretch.
   b) She was recovering from having her wisdom teeth extracted.
   c) She was pregnant with child.

3. What happened when they were in Bethlehem?
   a) Mary and Joseph went to the annual Carpenter's Union Dance.
   b) Mary went into labor and was about to give birth.
   c) Joseph was offered a good job, so he decided to stay there.

MEDITATION:

Both Joseph and Mary were descendants of King David, so they had to travel from Nazareth to Bethlehem in order to register for the census. (Joseph's genealogy is in Matthew 1:1-17 and Mary's genealogy is in Luke 3:23-38.)

For a description of what the journey must have been like, go to

http://jesustrail.com/blog/hiking-the-nativity-trail-from-nazareth-to-bethlehem

What a hassle! Especially since it was very close to the time when Mary would give birth. But many prophesies that include Bethlehem as the Messiah's birthplace were fulfilled because Joseph and Mary were obedient and traveled to Bethlehem.

We all go through hassles. That shouldn't keep us from being open to letting God work through us in our daily ups and downs.

Think of some hassles you're going through during this hectic holiday season and ask God to guide you through them as you continue to live each day and each moment focused on Jesus.

December 24

First read the entire passage — Luke 2:7-20.

She gave birth to her firstborn son. She wrapped him in bands of cloth, and laid him in a feeding trough, because there was no room for them in the inn.

There were shepherds in the same country staying in the field, and keeping watch by night over their flock. Behold, an angel of the Lord stood by them, and the glory of the Lord shone around them, and they were terrified. The angel said to them, "Don't be afraid, for behold, I bring you good news of great joy which will be to all the people. For there is born to you today, in David's city, a Savior, who is Christ the Lord. This is the sign to you: you will find a baby wrapped in strips of cloth, lying in a feeding trough."

Suddenly, there was with the angel a multitude of the heavenly army praising God, and saying, "Glory to God in the highest, on earth peace, good will toward men." When the angels went away from them into the sky, the shepherds said to one another, "Let's go to Bethlehem, now, and see this thing that has happened, which the Lord has made known to us." They came with haste, and found both Mary and Joseph, and the baby was lying in the feeding trough.

When they saw it, they publicized widely the saying which was spoken to them about this child. All who heard it wondered at the things which were spoken to them by the shepherds. But Mary kept all these sayings, pondering them in her heart. The shepherds returned, glorifying and praising God for all the things that they had heard and seen, just as it was told them.

Now re-read verse 7.

> She gave birth to her firstborn son. She wrapped him in bands of cloth, and laid him in a feeding trough, because there was no room for them in the inn.

1. Finally! The main event we've been waiting for, which is:
   a) Mary gives birth to her baby.
   b) Noah finishes the ark.
   c) Moses leads the Israelites into the promised land.

2. Where did Mary lay her baby?
   a) In a special bed for Jewish babies.
   b) On a large, soft pillow.
   c) In a feeding trough for animals.

Now re-read verses 8-12.

> There were shepherds in the same country staying in the field, and keeping watch by night over their flock. Behold, an angel of the Lord stood by them, and the glory of the Lord shone around them, and they were terrified. The angel said to them, "Don't be afraid, for behold, I bring you good news of great joy which will be to all the people. For there is born to you today, in David's city, a Savior, who is Christ the Lord. This is the sign to you: you will find a baby wrapped in strips of cloth, lying in a feeding trough."

1. To whom does the angel appear?
   a) King Herod
   b) Some shepherds
   c) The innkeeper

2. The angel has good news which will bring joy to whom?
   a) The Jews
   b) All people
   c) The shepherds and Mary

3. What IS this good news?
   a) The person who can save us has been born!
   b) We'll never go hungry, because God is going to make the Romans feed and clothe the rest of the world!
   c) Scientists just discovered the cure for the common cold!

4. How will the shepherds recognize the Messiah?
   a) He is a baby and He is lying in a basket.
   b) He is a baby and He is lying in an animal's feeding trough.
   c) He is a baby and He is wearing a blue cape with the letter "S" sewed on it.

Now re-read verses 13-16.

> Suddenly, there was with the angel a multitude of the heavenly army praising God, and saying, "Glory to God in the highest, on earth peace, good will toward men." When the angels went away from them into the sky, the shepherds said to one another, "Let's go to Bethlehem, now, and see this thing that has happened, which the Lord has made known to us." They came with haste, and found both Mary and Joseph, and the baby was lying in the feeding trough.

1. Who appears with the angel to praise God?
   a) Mary and Joseph and John the Baptist
   b) The three wise men
   c) A whole bunch of angels

2. Which of these three answers is the closest to the FIRST thing they all say?
   a) Yay God!
   b) Repent and be saved!
   c) Three cheers for John the Baptist!

3. The angels then say that God's peace will be with whom?
   a) All the little children
   b) Everyone except tax collectors
   c) Those who live on Earth.

4. What do the shepherds do when the angels leave them?
   a) They go to King Herod and tell him what the angels said.
   b) They go as fast as they can to find the Savior.
   c) They wait two days until the weather is good and then go to find Mary and Joseph.

Now re-read verses 17-20.

> When they saw it, they publicized widely the saying which was spoken to them about this child. All who heard it wondered at the things which were spoken to them by the shepherds. But Mary kept all these sayings, pondering them in her heart. The shepherds returned, glorifying and praising God for all the things that they had heard and seen, just as it was told them.

1. What do the shepherds do when they find Mary and Joseph?
   a) They rent a room at the inn for them.
   b) They help them escape from King Herod.
   c) They tell everyone what the angels told them about Jesus.

2. What do the shepherds do on their way home?
   a) They sing praises to God.
   b) They stop in Nazareth to tell Elizabeth and Zacharias the news of Jesus' birth.
   c) They stop at McDonald's for some hot chocolate.

MEDITATION:

The angels of the Lord announced their Good News to shepherds — ordinary people like you and me.

God still wants to introduce ordinary people like you and me to Jesus — God's son, our Savior.

DECEMBER 25

First read the entire passage — John 1:1-14.

Here's some background before you read:

The Gospel of John was written by John who was one of the twelve disciples. Mark 1:16-20 describes when John chose to follow Jesus. Luke 6:13-16 lists all twelve disciples.

In the beginning was the Word, and the Word was with God, and the Word was God. The same was in the beginning with God. All things were made through him. Without him was not anything made that has been made. In him was life, and the life was the light of men. The light shines in the darkness, and the darkness hasn't overcome it.

There came a man, sent from God, whose name was John. The same came as a witness, that he might testify about the light, that all might believe through him. He was not the light, but was sent that he might testify about the light. The true light that enlightens everyone was coming into the world.

He was in the world, and the world was made through him, and the world didn't recognize him. He came to his own, and those who were his own didn't receive him. But as many as received him, to them he gave the right to become God's children, to those who believe in his name: who were born not of blood, nor of the will of the flesh, nor of the will of man, but of God.

The Word became flesh, and lived among us. We saw his glory, such glory as of the one and only Son of the Father, full of grace and truth.

Now re-read verses 1-5.

> In the beginning was the Word, and the Word was with God, and the Word was God. The same was in the beginning with God. All things were made through him. Without him was not anything made that has been made. In him was life, and the life was the light of men. The light shines in the darkness, and the darkness hasn't overcome it.

1. The Gospel of John starts with these words:
   a) And it came to pass....
   b) In the beginning....
   c) Once upon a time....

2. The Gospel of John calls Jesus the Word . When did the Word exist?
   a) Since before time began — In the beginning WAS the Word.
   b) On the seventh day — God blessed the seventh day and made it holy.
   c) On Christmas day — She gave birth to a son and he gave him the name Jesus.

3. How does John describe Jesus?
   a) The light shining in the darkness.
   b) The voice crying in the wilderness.
   c) The wind beneath our wings.

Now re-read verses 6-9.

In verses 6-9 John refers to another John — John the Baptist, the cousin of Jesus, who was to prepare the way for the Lord.

> There came a man, sent from God, whose name was John. The same came as a witness, that he might testify about the light, that all might believe through him. He was not the light, but was sent that he might testify about the light. The true light that enlightens everyone was coming into the world.

1. Why did John the Baptist preach about Jesus?
   a) So that God might give him a promotion.
   b) So that his mother Elizabeth might be proud of him.
   c) So that every person might believe in Jesus.

Now re-read verses 10-13.

> He was in the world, and the world was made through him, and the world didn't recognize him. He came to his own, and those who were his own didn't receive him. But as many as received him, to them he gave the right to become God's children, to those who believe in his name: who were born not of blood, nor of the will of the flesh, nor of the will of man, but of God.

1. What happens to you when you believe in Jesus?
   a) You become a child of God.
   b) You become a missionary.
   c) You become immune to sin.

Now re-read verse 14.

> The Word became flesh, and lived among us. We saw his glory, such glory as of the one and only Son of the Father, full of grace and truth.

1. What do you think this means — *The Word became flesh and lived among us.*
   a) Sticks and stones will break my bones, but words will never harm me.
   b) Some dictionaries have leather covers (made of cow hides) at your local library.
   c) Jesus became a human being and lived on Earth.

MEDITATION:

So this is it — Christmas Day — the day we've been looking forward to ever since we started this Advent Bible Study 24 days ago.

Today we see The Baby lying in a manger in nativity sets, Christmas cards, tree ornaments, church bulletins, holiday books, and even TV commercials.

So the final question is this: Who do YOU see in that manger?

a) The Messiah that prophets predicted hundreds of years before His birth.
b) The Savior whom God promised to send, who will save us from our sins.
c) The Wonderful Counselor, Mighty God, Eternal Father, and Prince of Peace.
d) God's only Son.
e) The Light of the world.
f) Our Redeemer.

The answer should be: ALL OF THE ABOVE!

O come, let us adore Him.
O come, let us adore Him.
O come let us adore Him — Christ the Lord!

Your suggestions and feedback are invaluable!

Please reach out through www.fermatahouse.com.

Answers

DECEMBER 1

Verses 5-7

1b. King Herod was the king of Judea at that time.

2a. Zacharias was a priest.

3a. Elizabeth and Zacharias were childless when the angel visited Zacharias in the temple.

Verses 8-10

1b. Zacharias burned incense in the temple of the Lord.

2c. The people were praying while they waited outside.

Verses 11-14

1b. An angel came into the temple to talk to Zacharias.

2c. Zacharias thought he was alone and the angel startled him.

3b. The angel told Zacharias that he and Elizabeth were going to have a child.

4b. God wants Zacharias and Elizabeth to name the baby "John."

Verses 15-17

1a. John will be filled with the Holy Spirit before he's born.

2b. God wants John to help the children of God turn back to Him.

DECEMBER 2

Review

1a. Zacharias was in the temple.

2a. In December 1's Scripture (Luke 1:5-17), the angel's good news was that Zacharias and Elizabeth would have a baby.

Verses 18-20

1c. The angel's name is Gabriel.

2a. Zacharias' big mistake was that he didn't believe the angel of the Lord's message.

3a. Zacharias thought that he and Elizabeth were too old to have a baby.

Verses 21-22

1b. Zacharias couldn't talk.

Verses 23-25

1a. Elizabeth becomes pregnant (her baby is John the Baptist).

DECEMBER 3

Verses 26-27

1a. Verses 26-27 tell us of Gabriel's visit to Mary.

2b. Mary and Joseph are engaged at the time of Gabriel's visit.

3a. Joseph is a descendant of King David.

Verses 28-33

1a. Gabriel tells Mary that she's going to have a baby.

2a. God wants Mary to name the baby "Jesus."

3c. Mary's baby will be a king.

Verses 34-35

1b. Mary thinks she can't have a baby because she is still a virgin.

2c. God will perform a miracle so that Mary can have a baby.

3a. Jesus will be the Son of God.

Verses 36-38

1c. Nothing will be impossible with God.

2a. Mary tells Gabriel that she'll do the will of God.

DECEMBER 4

Verse 6

1a. This child is Jesus.

2a. Isaiah describes Jesus as "Wonderful, Counselor, Mighty God, Everlasting Father, Prince of Peace.

Verse 7

1b. Verse 7 describes what the world will be like when Jesus is King.

2a. The zeal of the Lord will enable Jesus to be the King.

DECEMBER 5

Review

1a. The angel tells Mary that she will be the mother of the Son of God.

2c. The angel also tells Mary that Elizabeth is also going to have a son.

3a. Elizabeth's husband is Zacharias.

4b. Elizabeth's son will be named "John."

Verses 39-41

1b. Mary went to visit Elizabeth.

2c. Elizabeth was filled with the Holy Spirit upon Mary's arrival.

Verses 42-45

1b. Elizabeth proclaims that God has blessed Mary in a very special way.

2b. Mary is blessed because she believed God's promise that she will be the mother of the Son of God.

DECEMBER 6

Verse 46

1b. Mary is speaking in verse 46.

2a. Mary is speaking to Elizabeth in verse 46.

3b. Mary begins her speech by praising God.

Verses 47-49

1c. Mary says that people from all future generations will know her as the one whom God blessed.

2a. Mary says that God has been terrific to her and has done wonderful things for her.

3c. Mary says that God's name is Holy.

Verses 50-53

1b. In verses 50-53, Mary says that God helps the poor and humble.

Verses 54-56

1b. Mary mentions Abraham because God promised Abraham that He would send help for the Israelites. [Genesis 12:1-3]

2c. Mary stays with Elizabeth three months.

DECEMBER 7

Review

1b. Zacharias is Elizabeth's husband.

2a. Zacharias can't talk because he didn't believe what the angel Gabriel told him.

3b. Elizabeth is to name her son "John."

4b. John's mission will be to help God's children turn back to Him.

Verses 57-60

1c. Elizabeth's friends wanted to name her baby "Zacharias," after his father.

2c. Elizabeth told her friends that the baby's name will be "John."

Verses 61-63

1b. Zacharias and Elizabeth's friends object to naming the baby "John," because none of their relatives are named "John."

2a. Zacharias had to write the name because he still couldn't talk.

DECEMBER 8

Review

1b. Zacharias wrote the name "John" on a writing tablet.

Verses 64-66

1c. After Zacharias wrote down the name that the angel Gabriel had told him, he was able to speak again.

2a. Immediately after Zacharias was able to speak, he praised God.

3b. The people thought that the Lord was with Zacharias and Elizabeth's baby John in a very special way.

Verses 67-69

1a. Zacharias is speaking in verses 67-69. He is the father of John the Baptist.

2b. Zacharias is praising God for providing the Israelites a person who will save them and set them free.

3a. The deliverer that Zacharias is speaking of will be a descendant of King David.

4b. The deliverer in Zacharias' prophesy is Jesus.

Verses 70-75

1c. God promised to deliver the Israelites from their enemies so that they would be free to serve God without fear.

2a. God made this promise of deliverance to Abraham. [Genesis 12]

DECEMBER 9

Review

1b. The first part of Zacharias' prophecy in verses 67-75 talks about God sending us a deliverer.

Verse 76

1a. In the second part of Zacharias' prophecy, he talks about his son, John (whom we know as John the Baptist).

2c. John will grow up to be a prophet of the Lord.

3a. John's life mission will be to prepare the way for our Lord Jesus.

Verses 77-80

1b. Our sins are forgiven by the tender mercy of our God.

2c. The tender mercy of our God guides our feet into the way of peace.

3b. John got strong in the Spirit of the Lord.

DECEMBER 10

Verses 1-2

1b. Pontius Pilate was governor of Judea when John the Baptist was living in the wilderness.

2a. John the Baptist is the main character in Luke 3.

3b. Zacharias is the father of John the Baptist.

Verse 3

1c. John baptized people who wanted to show that they were repenting of their sins.

2a. The people wanted to receive the baptism of repentance for the forgiveness of their sins.

Verses 4-6

1c. Luke quotes from the 40th chapter of Isaiah, the prophet.

2b. Luke quotes Isaiah because John the Baptist's life fulfills this prophecy.

3b. The rough parts will be made smooth.

4b. The rough parts represent our frailties, like loneliness, guilt, and lack of hope, to name a few.

5b. All people on earth will see God's salvation and deliverance.

DECEMBER 11

Verses 7-8

1b. When John the Baptist calls the people vipers, he's insulting them.

2a. John the Baptist was angry at the people because they acted like they didn't need to repent from their sins.

3a. The people thought they didn't need to repent from their sins because they were descendants of Abraham, whom God blessed.

Verses 9-11

1c. If our lives do not bear fruit, we will be cut off from God.

2a. John the Baptist tells the people to share what they have with those in need.

Verses 12-14

1c. John the Baptist advises the tax collectors to collect no more than the legal amount.

2b. John the Baptist advises the soldiers to not accuse anyone wrongfully.

Verses 15-17

1b. The people thought John the Baptist might be the Messiah.

2a. The person who John the Baptist is preparing them for will baptize them in the Holy Spirit and fire.

DECEMBER 12

Verses 7-8

1b. The commandment is for us to love one another.

2a. Love is of God.

3c. He who doesn't love doesn't know God.

4c. God is love.

Verses 9-11

1a. God sent his one and only Son into the world.

2b. God sent his Son that we might live through him.

Verses 12-13

1a. If we love one another, God lives in us.

Verses 14-15

1c. God has sent his Son as the Savior of the world.

2a. If you tell others that Jesus is the Son of God, then God will live in you and you will live in God.

DECEMBER 13

Verses 18-19

1a. Mary, the mother of Jesus, was engaged to Joseph.

2a. Joseph had intended to divorce Mary quietly and help her get out of town.

Verses 20-21

1b. Joseph changed his mind when an angel appeared to him in a dream.

2a. The angel describes Mary's baby as a miracle of the Holy Spirit.

3c. The angel tells Joseph that Mary's baby is to be named "Jesus."

4b. Jesus is the one who will save God's people from their sins.

Verses 22-23

1b. Immanuel means "God with us."

Verses 24-25

1a. When Joseph woke up, he did everything the angel commanded him.

DECEMBER 14

Verse 5

1a. God is sending someone who will reign as king.

2b. This king will be a descendant of King David.

3a. This king will deal wisely and rule fairly.

Verse 6

1c. The Israelites shall dwell safely when the Messiah rules as king.

2b. This king shall be called: Yahweh our righteousness. (Many translations of the Bible use the word *Lord* as a substitute for *Yahweh*)

3b. This is Jeremiah's prophecy of the Messiah, who is Jesus.

DECEMBER 15

Verses 4-5

1b. A woman gave birth to the Son of God.

2c. God sent us his son in the fullness of time.

3a. God's son was born under the Jewish Law so that he might redeem those who are under the Law.

4a. God's son redeems us so that we might be adopted as children of God.

Verses 6-7

1a. When we are children of God, we have the Holy Spirit in our hearts.

2a. Our hearts cry out "Abba, Father" when we become children of God.

3b. When Jesus redeems us, we are no longer bondservants — we are children of God.

DECEMBER 16

Verses 1-4

1c. Each of the young women carry their lamps as they go out to meet the bridegroom.

2b. The five foolish girls didn't pack any oil for their lamps.

3a. The five wise girls packed oil for their lamps.

Verses 5-7

1b. All ten girls fell asleep while they waited for the bridegroom.

2a. When the ten girls hear that the bridegroom is coming, they prepare their lamps.

Verses 8-9

1c. The foolish girls ask the wise girls for some oil.

2b. The wise girls tell the foolish girls that they don't have enough oil to share, and they suggest that the foolish girls find someone who sells oil.

Verses 10-13

1b. The bridegroom arrives when the foolish girls are gone away to buy some oil for their lamps.

2a. The girls who are prepared go to the marriage feast with the bridegroom.

3c. When the foolish girls try to attend the marriage feast, they are not allowed in.

4a. In this parable, Jesus makes the point that we need to always be ready. The Messiah could come again at any time.

DECEMBER 17

Verse 1

1b. The introduction of the genealogy of Jesus mentions David and Abraham.

Verse 6

1a. Jesse is King David's father.

Isaiah 11:1-2

1c. Isaiah uses the image of a branch when he describes the relationship between Jesse and the Messiah.

Verse 16

1b. Joseph is the last man mentioned in this genealogy of Jesus.

2a. This genealogy of Jesus lists Mary as his mother.

DECEMBER 18

Verse 1

1c. Jesse is King David's father.

Jeremiah 33:15

1a. Jeremiah and Isaiah refer to the Messiah as a branch.

Verses 2-5

1a. The seven-fold spirit includes Yahweh's Spirit, the spirit of wisdom, understanding, counsel, power, knowledge, and the fear of Yahweh. (Remember – many translations of the Bible use the word *Lord* in place of *Yahweh.*)

2c. Righteousness and faithfulness will be the belt of his waist.

Verses 6-9

1b. When the earth is full of the knowledge of the Lord, then there will be peace.

Verse 10

1b. Isaiah refers to the Messiah as "the root of Jesse."

2a. Jesse is King David's father.

3a. Jesus is a descendant of Jesse.

DECEMBER 19

Verse 16

1b. For God so loved the world that he gave his one and only Son.

2a. Whoever believes in God will have eternal life.

Verses 17-18

1c. God didn't send his Son into the world to judge the world, but that the world should be saved through him.

2a. He who believes in God's Son is not judged.

3a. He who doesn't believe in God's Son has been judged already.

Verses 19-21

1c. Everyone who does evil hates the light and avoids the light so that his evil works won't be exposed.

2b. Everyone who does good and loves Truth comes to the light so that his works may be revealed, since they have been done in God.

DECEMBER 20

Verses 25-26

1b. Simeon was a righteous and devout man.

2c. The Holy Spirit had revealed to Simeon that he would not die until he had met the Messiah.

Verses 27-32

1b. The Spirit led Simeon into the temple.

2a. Mary and Joseph brought Jesus to the temple to comply with the Jewish law.

3b. Simeon held Jesus in his arms and said that he had seen God's salvation.

4a. Simeon refers to Jesus as God's light for revelation to the Gentiles and God's light of glory for the Jews.

Verses 33-35

1b. Joseph and Mary were marveling at the things which Simeon spoke.

2b. Simeon prophesizes that Mary will experience much sadness. Of course, we know that about thirty-three years later she experienced much sadness when her son was crucified.

DECEMBER 21

Verse 2 of Micah 5

1b. Micah prophesies that the Messiah will be born in Bethlehem Ephratah.

Verses 5-6 of Matthew 2

1c. The Wise Men quote Micah 5:2.

Verses 3-4 of Micah 5

1a. Micah describes the Messiah as a shepherd.

Verse 11 of John 10

1c. Jesus describes himself as *The Good Shepherd*.

DECEMBER 22

Verses 19-20

1c. The religious leaders confronted John the Baptist.

2b. The religious leaders asked John the Baptist *Who are you?*

3a. John the Baptist answers, *I am not the Christ.*

Verses 21-22

1c. The religious leaders wonder if John the Baptist is Elijah.

2a. John the Baptist tells the religious leaders that he is not Elijah.

Verse 23

1c. John the Baptist quotes from the book of Isaiah the prophet.

Isaiah 40:3

1a. John the Baptist claims to be the voice of one crying in the wilderness, "Make straight the way of the Lord."

John 1:24-28

1b. John the Baptist baptizes in water.

2a. John the Baptist was baptizing near the Jordan river when the religious leaders confronted him.

DECEMBER 23

Verses 1-3

1a. A decree went out from Caesar Augustus that all the world should be enrolled.

2b. Quirinius was the governor of Syria at this time.

3a. Everyone went to his own city of origin for the census.

Verse 4

1b. Joseph was in the city of Nazareth in Galilee when he heard the news about the census.

2a. Joseph must enroll for the census in Bethlehem, which is in Judea.

3c. Joseph must enroll for the census in Bethlehem, since he is a descendant of David.

Verses 5-6

1b. Mary traveled with Joseph to Bethlehem to register for the census.

2c. Mary was pregnant when she and Joseph traveled to Bethlehem.

3b. While Mary and Joseph were in Bethlehem, she went into labor.

DECEMBER 24

Verse 7

1a. Mary gave birth to her firstborn son.

2c. Mary laid her baby in a feeing trough for animals.

Verses 8-12

1b. An angel of the Lord appeared to shepherds in the field.

2b. The angel has good news of great joy which will be to ALL the people.

3a. The angel brings the good news that our Savior has been born.

4b. The angel tells the shepherds that the Messiah is lying in a feeding trough.

Verses 13-16

1c. A multitude of the heavenly army of angels appeared.

2a. The angels say *Glory to God in the highest* which is kind of like saying *Yay God!*

3c. The angels say *On earth peace, good will toward men.*

4b. The shepherds went with haste to find Mary and Joseph and the Savior.

Verses 17-20

1c. The shepherds publicized widely the saying which the angel told them about this child.

2a. The shepherds returned, glorifying and praising God.

DECEMBER 25

Verses 1-5

1b. The opening words of the Gospel of John are *In the beginning*.

2a. *The Word* existed before time began.

3a. John describes Jesus as the light shining in the darkness.

Verses 6-9

1c. John the Baptist testified about Jesus so that all might believe.

Verses 10-13

1a. Jesus gave the right to become God's children to those who believe in his name.

Verse 14

1c. Jesus became a human being and lived on Earth.

JOIN THE TEAM

You can help improve the *Choose This Day Multiple Choice Bible Study Series* by sending your **comments** to www.fermatahouse.com/contact/.

And you can help make the Series more accessible to others by leaving a **review** on amazon.com. Amazon's search engine has an algorithm for visibility which is largely based on the number of **reviews** a book receives. Just a few words will suffice.

Thanks in advance!

ALSO FROM FERMATA HOUSE...

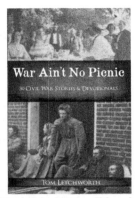

War Ain't No Picnic: 30 Civil War Stories & Devotionals

Award-winning storyteller and Methodist pastor, Tom Letchworth, retells some of the most fascinating stories from the American Civil War.

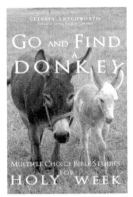

Go and Find a Donkey: Multiple Choice Bible Studies for Holy Week

Go and Find a Donkey is the second installment of the *Choose This Day Multiple Choice Bible Studies* series.

Getting Ready for Christmas Word Search Puzzles for Advent

Use this entertaining and challenging word search puzzle book to immerse your brain in the Bible passages associated with the coming of the Messiah.

The unique "No-Spoiler Solution" pages that are found in all of Fermata House's word search puzzle books help make the puzzles accessible for all ages and skill levels. They include hints *and* solutions.

Made in the USA
Middletown, DE
21 November 2022

15644827R00076